VOICES FROM THE FEDERAL THEATRE

*Bonnie Nelson Schwartz
and the Educational Film Center*

Foreword by Robert Brustein

UNIVERSITY OF WISCONSIN PRESS

1003696657 T

The University of Wisconsin Press
1930 Monroe Street
Madison, Wisconsin 53711

www.wisc.edu/wisconsinpress/

3 Henrietta Street
London WC2E 8LU, England

5   4   3   2   1

Printed in the United States of America

Library of Congress Cataloging-in-Publication Data
Schwartz, Bonnie Nelson.
   Voices from the Federal Theatre / Bonnie Nelson Schwartz and the
Educational Film Center; foreword by Robert Brustein.
      p.   cm.
   ISBN 0-299-18320-3 (hardcover: alk. paper)—ISBN 0-299-18324-6
(pbk.: alk. paper)
   1. Federal Theatre Project (U.S.) I. Educational Film Center
(Annandale, Va.) II. Title.
   PN2270.F43S38 2003
   792'.0973—dc21
                                                              2003007240

Terrace Books, a division of the University of Wisconsin Press, takes its
name from the Memorial Union Terrace, located at the Univeristy of
Wisconsin–Madison. Since its inception in 1907, the Wisconsin
Union has provided a venue for students, faculty, staff, and alumni to
debate art, music, politics, and the issues of the day. It is a place where
theatre, music, drama, dance, outdoor activities, and major speakers are
made available to the campus and the community. To learn more about
the Union, visit www.union.wisc.edu.

VOICES FROM THE
FEDERAL THEATRE

DATE DUF F

For David

ACKNOWLEDGMENTS

Bob Baker
Perry Bruskin
Jules Dassin
Clinton Turner Davis
Lincoln Diamant
Katherine Dunham
Richard Eyre
John Houseman
Woodie King, Jr.
Rosetta LeNoire
Norman Lloyd
Arthur Miller
Alan Peters
John Randolph
Robert Schnitzer
Studs Terkel
Virginia Wren
The National Endowment for the Humanities
The Corporation for Public Broadcasting
. . . and the hundreds of thousands of people who gave life to
the Federal Theatre Project

Also, Lorraine Brown, Ira H. Klugerman, Ruth Pollak,
Steven L. Rabin, Dan Wilcox

CONTENTS

III. THE WRITERS

IV. THE VARIETY ARTISTS

V. OTHER VOICES

HALLIE'S COMET: THE FEDERAL THEATRE

by Robert Brustein

The glorious, totally improbable, and ultimately ill-fated adventure known as the Federal Theatre Project lasted from 1935 to 1939.

It was killed by an act of Congress in an atmosphere of Red-baiting and political hysteria. Yet, in four short years not only did this visionary organization create a host of successful Federal Theatre productions, but it helped revolutionize our notions of the geography and purpose of the American stage.

Conceived in the middle of the Great Depression as a plan to find jobs for an estimated twenty to thirty thousand out-of-work actors, directors, playwrights, designers, and stagehands, the Federal Theatre at its height eventually employed thirteen thousand theatre artists in thirty-one states. The relief agency known as the Works Project Administration (WPA), under the enlightened leadership of President Franklin Delano Roosevelt's deputy Harry Hopkins, had come to realize that among the more than one-third of the nation that was ill-fed, ill-clad, and ill-housed were a number of indigent artists. Hopkins thereupon proceeded to organize a series of arts projects, including one for the theatre, and began looking around for an appropriate leader.

Hopkins found his ideal national director in Hallie Flanagan Davis, a forty-five-year-old professor of drama at Vassar who possessed boundless energy, irrepressible optimism, untiring zeal, and no administrative experience whatsoever. Hopkins knew instinctively that the project had to be run by a non–commercial theatre person, and Hallie had caught his eye through the experimental work she had been doing at Vassar. He was soon to learn that she was not only an extraordinary theatre visionary but an individual of unusual character, integrity, and drive—qualities that in combination made her one of the greatest leaders in the history of American theatre.

Rather than feeling her way into her new job, Hallie began with very clear ideas about what was expected of a federal theatre. She was convinced that such a project, though conceived as a source of economic relief, was obliged to establish and maintain high artistic standards. A subsidized federal theatre would have to be an alternative to the commercial stage, not a competitor with it, keeping ticket prices within the reach of all. It would also need to be a decentralized theatre—indeed, the seed of a national theatre movement—creating productions not just in New York but in every major city and region of the country. And as perhaps her most controversial idea, its mission would be to produce plays that were not mere entertainments but artworks relevant to the social and political problems of the day.

Each of these decisions was destined to extend the boundaries of the American stage, and each was destined to land the Federal Theatre in a lot of hot water. The attempt to combine relief and art, for example, was full of potential conflict, particularly because of the differing goals of social work and artistic achievement. Was the Federal Theatre to be a source of great plays and productions or rather an agency designed to better the lives of the unemployed? How could the Federal Theatre pursue the goals of excellence when the best American theatre artists were not among the unemployed—indeed, when Broadway producers sometimes wanted the same artists, at substantially higher wages, for their commercial shows?

Many of the same producers were criticizing the Federal Theatre's subsidized ticket prices (sometimes as low as 25 cents) as unfair competition for the higher-priced Broadway stage, but this was only one of Hallie's headaches. Her effort to decentralize the Federal Theatre, a highly successful move when measured by the number of new theatres being formed around the country in a very brief time, did not always produce work of the highest professional quality. Moreover, the effort sometimes stimulated narrow, regional prejudices and chauvinisms. Most dangerous of all, the social and political tub-thumping of the Federal Theatre made it consistently vulnerable to government censorship.

Harry Hopkins had promised Hallie a theatre that was "free, adult, uncensored." Too often he was unable to keep that pledge. This should not surprise us. There are few patrons of the arts, least of all the government, who have been able to refrain from meddling in the conduct of the artists they support, especially when their work has a high political profile. And there is no question that Federal Theatre artists, with Hallie's blessings, did not hesitate to embroil her in controversy.

Hallie was never opposed to using the theatre for propaganda purposes, if that meant exposing political corruption or unjust social conditions. Although she was often accused of promoting Communism and even of being a Communist herself, she never consciously allowed the Federal Theatre to be used for the purpose of endorsing political parties or advancing political aims. Indeed, she did not hesitate to cancel plays that seemed overtly partisan to her. As she wrote in a note chastising one of her more radical producers, "I will not have the Federal Theatre used politically. I will not have it used to further the ends of the Democratic party, the Republican party, or the Communist party."

The occasion was a production called *Injunction Granted*, a play about duped workers and rapacious capitalists that Hallie called "bad journalism and hysterical theatre" because it used government funds "as a party tool." It might have been disingenuous of her to believe that her goal of "a relevant theatre with regional roots," devoted to dramatizing social problems like homelessness and electrical power, would not be exploited for narrow political purposes. It might have been even more naive to assume that the agency that subsidized these productions would refrain from suppressing or censoring them if they threatened government interests.

The first government collision arose over a play called *Ethiopia* when the WPA banned the appearance on stage of such heads of state as Benito Mussolini and Haile Selassie (Robert Schnitzer's Delaware production of *Julius Caesar* was also castigated for insulting Il Duce). This move led to the resignation of Elmer Rice as director of the New York Project. There would be even more consternation when Federal Theatre productions criticized or ridiculed American political figures, an irresistible temptation considering the level of mind in Congress at the time.

Hallie began by dividing her empire into five large units: (1) the Living Newspaper; (2) popular price theatre, with Yiddish, Spanish, and other ethnic companies; (3) experimental theatre; (4) Negro theatre, under the

directorship of John Houseman and Rose McClendon; and (5) tryout theatre. Hallie's Living Newspapers were always destined to be the most
inflammatory things she produced. An effort to dramatize the news ("something like the *March of Time* in the movies," Harry Hopkins explained to a
belligerent congressman), the Living Newspaper was a spinoff of the epic
techniques of Brecht and Piscator. Using confrontational devices and
polemical themes, it was meant to be an antidote to a commercial theatre
that, in Hallie's words, "continues to tell in polite whispers its tales of small
triangular love stories in small rectangular settings." The Living Newspaper
settings, as designed by scenic artists like Howard Bay and Mordecai
Gorelik, making good use of George Izenour's new remote control switchboard, were imaginative and various. They substituted light and projections
for the "cumbersome scenery" that Hallie and other theatre visionaries were
now finding obsolete, mainly because "the cinema," as she added propheti-
cally, "had beaten realism at its own game."

More importantly, the stories told in these openly propagandistic pieces
concerned the big issues of the time. In the first of the Living Newspaper successes, *Triple-A Plowed Under*, the Federal Theatre enjoined the farmer and
the consumer to unite for higher wages and healthier food. It ran for eighty-
five performances in New York and was later produced in Chicago,
Cleveland, Los Angeles, and Milwaukee, though not in Texas, where a WPA
administrator exhorted Hallie to do "old plays" that didn't evoke bad criticism. That Texan bureaucrat might have had the same complaint about
Power, a call for public ownership of utilities; *Spirochete*, a history of syphilis
climaxing with a call for mandatory blood tests; and, unquestionably the
Federal Theatre's greatest success, *One Third of a Nation*, which exposed the
existence of poor housing conditions in the nation's largest cities.

The audience's appetite for "old plays," however, would seem to have
been satisfied by the Federal Theatre unit under the direction of John
Houseman and Orson Welles. But even classical production was not to be free
of controversy. These early efforts to deconstruct classics by making them
more "relevant" to the contemporary world (a process later employed by such
modern directors as Andrei Serban, Peter Brook, and Peter Sellars), successful as some of them were, still managed to raise hackles. Houseman had hired
Welles, then at the tender age of twenty, to direct *Macbeth* with his Negro
unit. Setting the play in Haiti, Welles turned the witches into voodoo witch
doctors and treated the central character as if he were "Emperor Jones gone

beautifully mad," thereby creating a triumph that played New York and toured the country to great acclaim. The success of this "Voodoo" Macbeth encouraged Negro units throughout the country to stage black versions of other European classics, such as The "Swing" Mikado and Lysistrata, though the latter was eventually shut down by the WPA for being too "risqué."

Following Macbeth, which was staged at the Lafayette Theatre in Harlem, Houseman and Welles took over the Maxine Elliot Theatre on Broadway to produce two more scintillating versions of classic plays: Horse Eats Hat, a wild adaptation of a nineteenth-century Labiche farce featuring the young Joseph Cotten, and Christopher Marlowe's Doctor Faustus, directed by and starring Welles in the title role (his first leading part in New York). Faustus was by all accounts a mesmerizing reinterpretation of a great classical play, with Jack Carter (the black actor who played Macbeth) turning Mephistopheles into a dignified, bemused portrait of evil. Welles meanwhile could indulge his weakness for heavy makeup along with his lifelong passion for magic in the way he staged the episode involving the Seven Deadly Sins.

The Federal Theatre was now on a roll. Critics were calling it the "greatest producer of hits" in New York. The best dramatists of the day, such as Bernard Shaw and Eugene O'Neill, delighted to get produced in regions that would normally never be exposed to their work, were letting the project do their plays for a royalty of $50 a week or less. Similarly, novelists, like Sinclair Lewis, were only too happy to accept Hallie's invitation to adapt their novels into plays. Lewis's It Can't Happen Here, about the coming of fascism to America, though a poor piece of dramatic writing, had twenty-two productions opening simultaneously in eighteen cities and played to nearly five hundred thousand people. Inevitably, the play was interpreted as campaign propaganda for the New Deal.

Despite its accumulating successes, however, the Federal Theatre suffered a grievous loss in authority and personnel when Marc Blitzstein's Brechtian satire The Cradle Will Rock was canceled by the WPA administration, on the eve of its opening, under the pretext of budget cutting. The story of the opera's clandestine resurrection is now too well known to require extensive retelling (that episode would be the centerpiece of Tim Robbins's 1999 film, also called The Cradle Will Rock, which starred Cherry Jones as Hallie Flanagan). Suffice it to say Welles and Houseman walked their opening-night audience twenty blocks uptown from the Maxine Elliot to the empty Venice Theatre; Blitzstein played the entire score from his piano; and the actors, cleverly skirting a union injunction, sang their parts from the house, all to thunderous applause.

But it was a Pyrrhic victory for the Federal Theatre. Welles and Houseman left the project soon after to form their own Mercury Theatre, where they produced a groundbreaking *Julius Caesar* in black shirt and a mesmerizing *Heartbreak House*, which found the twenty-two-year-old Welles once again applying excessive makeup to play the octagnerian Captain Shotover. Although Hallie professed to be happy whenever her artists found work in the commercial theatre, the Houseman-Welles defection left her without her two most dynamic figures and valuable assets.

She was also losing her greatest supporter in the Roosevelt administration, Harry Hopkins, who, ill with cancer, was starting to let less-informed assistants make his decisions for him. (The quality of those decisions can be assessed by the opinion of one of them, a California bureaucrat, who called a good theatre project "anything that keeps out of the papers.") In his second term, Roosevelt had cut government spending in order to avoid inflation and give business a leg up. As usual, the first area to suffer was the arts.

Around this time Hallie remained resolutely focused on her mandate to create a truly national theatre, making tireless tours of the country in an effort to ensure that all the regional units were running well and maintaining high standards. Wherever she went, she encountered gratitude from artists and audiences alike, but also hostility from some of the press and abuse from some of the politicians. There was the usual criticism growing in Congress that too much money was being spent in New York by Bolshevik sympathizers. The *Washington Post* called for an end of the Federal Theatre and its "frilly artistic projects." William Randolph Hearst's *San Francisco Examiner* carried a headline demanding, "Federal Theatre Communist Trend Must Be Eradicated." One Congressional investigator was appalled that in some Federal Theatre shows, blacks and whites shared the same stage and even "danced together." Even the titles of harmless Federal Theatre stock farces—*The Bishop Misbehaves, Up in Mabel's Room, Lend Me Your Husband*—were being denounced as lewd and salacious by congressmen who never bothered to see the plays.

It must be admitted that the Workers' Alliance, a socialist organization said to be a nursery for the Communist Party, was recruiting a lot of Federal Theatre employees. And it is also true that some of the project's later work, notably the children's play *Revolt of the Beavers*, was sufficiently slanted to provoke the *New York Times*'s Brooks Atkinson into saying it was Karl Marx disguised as Mother Goose, and the *Saturday Evening Post* into charging the Federal Theatre with teaching poor children to murder rich ones (actually, kids of all income brackets loved the show as a story of good guys versus bad guys). Hallie often replied, with a zealousness that knew no fear, that only a free people could create a Federal Theatre, that it was a democratic answer both to communism and fascism. But no one seemed to be listening. The Federal Theatre, lacking any genuine grassroots support, was being convicted without defense in the court of public opinion.

Eventually, the House Un-American Activities Committee, under the chairmanship of the notorious Martin Dies of Texas, saw the political controversy engulfing the Federal Theatre as an excellent opportunity to attack the Roosevelt administration. Dies's fellow committeeman from New Jersey, J. Parnell Thomas—both of them would soon turn their attention in the direction of "Reds" in Hollywood—identified the Federal Theatre not just as a "link in the vast and unparalleled New Deal propaganda machine" but as an arm of the Communist Party. In the words of Jane De Hart Matthews (*The Federal Theatre, 1935–39*), "Hereafter, Hallie Flanagan would find her time and attention devoted increasingly to defense of the Federal Theatre, rather than to its expansion."

Hallie's preoccupation with defending the reputation of her enterprise would also occupy the attention of the best commentators on the subject—not only Ms. De Hart but, as she admitted in her poignant and powerful memoir, *Arena*, Hallie herself. As a drama with its own heroes and villains, this conflict between strong-arm politics and defenseless art was a natural for press attention, but its outcome was foreordained. Not only would the Democratic administration fail to put through its projected plan for a new governmental Department of Art, providing subsidized theatrical, musical, and art activities in twenty-five to one hundred cities; it would be enjoined from supporting any art at all, especially the art of the theatre.

What is deeply frustrating about this encounter is that for many months the eloquent Hallie Flanagan was prevented by the WPA administration from releasing any statements to the press in her own defense. She had to remain silent in the face of criticism not only of her own politics but of the Federal Theatre's artistic achievements. Witness after witness testified to how the Federal Theatre was dominated by Communists and fellow travelers, after which Representative Clifton Woodrum of Virginia informed the House that the Federal Theatre "has produced nothing of merit as far as national productions are concerned," adding with smug pride, "We are going out of the theatre business."

Finally, Hallie was allowed to submit a brief before the Dies Committee, but only after a large number of unfriendly witnesses had sufficiently tarnished the reputation of her endeavor. The brief was never read or published, but some of it was covered in her testimony. She began by defending, first, the patriotism of her project ("Since August 29, 1935, I have been . . . combating un-American activity"), and then herself against charges that because she had once visited Russia and written favorably about Russian theatre, she was a Red. It is disheartening to find this dignified human being forced to say "that I am not and never have been a Communist; that I am a registered Democrat, . . . that I had planned and directed Federal Theatre from the first as an American enterprise." Words of a similar nature would echo and re-echo throughout Congressional chambers for many years to come.

Hallie was willing to concede that many of her productions were expressions of propaganda, but she insisted that propaganda was a form of education for democracy, rather than a tool for advancing Communist doctrine. In a moment that summed up the nature of this investigation, she was asked by Representative Joe Starnes (D-AL) about an ominous figure named Christopher Marlowe. "You are quoting from this Marlowe. Is he a Communist?" "Put in the record," Hallie replied, "that he was the greatest dramatist in the period of Shakespeare." It was a blunder on a level with the HUAC charge some years later that the eight-year-old Shirley Temple was a communist for dancing with Bill Robinson, and it was a blunder that would end up in Starnes's obituary, though unfortunately not on his tombstone.

But Hallie could make no impact on a committee determined to extinguish the Federal Theatre from the face of the earth. With Chairman Dies raising his gavel to end the hearings for lunch, Hallie asked to be allowed to make a final statement. Dies said he would consider it, but she never got her chance to be heard again, nor was her testimony ever distributed. "We don't want you back," declared Congressman Thomas, "You're a tough customer, and we're all worn out."

As a direct result of these hearings, the House eventually passed, by a vote of 373 to 21, the Relief Bill for 1939–40, calling for sweeping changes in the WPA program, including drastic cuts in arts funding and the imposition of loyalty oaths designed to get rid of radicals. It also called for an end to the Federal Theatre. Hallie learned about this development from a newspaper someone handed her, shocked that Congress had decided on what she called "outright execution rather than slow strangulation."

There would be rallies on behalf of the Federal Theatre. Critics would speak of its great achievements. Orson Welles would offer to debate hostile politicians on radio. Telegrams would pour in from far and wide. And the Senate, charmed by Tallulah Bankhead, daughter of one of its members, would briefly consider keeping the Federal Theatre alive for a few more years. But the effort failed because the Senate was reluctant to put other artists out of work in order to save funds for the Federal Theatre, and, for the same reason, Roosevelt sadly signed the bill.

Despite Hallie's brave cries of "Do not give up!" and the thunderous support of the entire theatre industry and thousands of supporters, all efforts to save the Federal Theatre proved of no avail. This first attempt in history to subsidize serious American theatre with federal funds was treated by Congress with the same hostility, maliciousness, and fear that were later to surround the National Endowment for the Arts, and a great Idea, one that brought fine theatre to a new audience of millions of Americans, fell victim to narrow and bigoted minds.

"Thus Federal Theatre ended as it began," wrote Hallie in *Arena,* "with fearless presentation of problems touching American life. If this first government theatre in our country had been less alive it might have lived longer. But I do not believe anyone who worked on it regrets that it stood from first to last against reaction, against prejudice, against racial, religious, and political intolerance. It strove for a more dramatic statement and a better understanding of the great forces of our life today; it fought for a free theatre as one of the many expressions of a civilized, informed, and vigorous life."

Hallie not only lost her job; she lost her second husband, Philip H. Davis, soon after the demise of the Federal Theatre. She went back to academic life in 1941, accepting a position at Smith College as dean and as professor of drama. It was there that as a student at Amherst, I first met her, when one of my Smith girlfriends was playing in a Living Newspaper piece called $E=mc^2$ about the splitting of the atom. Four years later Hallie developed the illness that seems to afflict so many theatre artists, Parkinson's disease, and retired to her old haunts in Poughkeepsie near Vassar, where she died in 1969 at the age of seventy-nine.

The Voices of the Federal Theatre, some of them growing a little hoarse and parched with age, all testify to the vigor, the energy, the controversy, and the fearlessness that characterized this project and its leader. Reflecting the ephemeral nature of the theatre itself, nothing remains of the productions except for some faded photographs and some yellowing scripts. But just as other federal arts projects produced such giants as John Cheever, Ralph Ellison and Richard Wright in the Writers' program, and Jackson Pollock, Willem De Kooning, Philip Guston, and Jack Levine in the Art Project, the Theatre program provided a home for some of the most brilliant actors, directors, designers, and dancers of the period (only the Group Theatre can boast as many gifted alumni): Orson Welles and John Houseman, Norman Lloyd, Arthur Kennedy, Katherine Dunham, Helen Tamiris, Jack Carter, Canada Lee, Ian Keith, Joseph Cotten, Burt Lancaster, Sidney Lumet, E.G. Marshall, Alvin Childress, Will Geer, Paula Lawrence, John Randolph, Jules Dassin, Jose Limon—the list is endless. And this in the face of the fact that the Federal Theatre was mandated to hire not reigning stars but primarily the unemployed.

But let the last words be those of the great woman who saw this project through those four exhilarating, demoralizing, incomparable years: "The President of the United States in writing to me of his regret at the closing of the Federal Theatre referred to it as a pioneering job. This it was, gutsy, lusty, bad and good, sad and funny, superbly worth more wit, wisdom and imagination than we could give it. Its significance lies in pointing to the future. The ten thousand anonymous men and women—the et ceteras and the and-so-forths who did the work, the nobodies who were everybody, the somebodies who believed it—their dreams and deeds were not the end. They were the beginning of a people's theatre in a country whose greatest plays are still to come."

Those of us in the serious American theatre have built on the back of this brave enterprise and in the shadow of the unconquerable figure who led it. May her spirit rest unperturbed and proud.

PREFACE

Naturally, if you get a few actors, a few theatre people together and give them a roof over their heads and enough to eat, they're liable to create miracles, which is exactly what happened.

John Houseman

What is it like to recall a time some 70 years ago, a time that was fraught with the pain and hardship of Depression-ridden America, yet a time when you were young and strong-headed and the fever ran high? In the words of Studs Terkel, it was a time framed by "the holocaust of the Great Depression."

This book is about its survivors—the men and women of the 1930s' Federal Theatre Project, a government relief measure that brought more theatre to more people, in every corner of America, than at any time in history. It was killed in a firestorm of controversy that gave birth to the damning question "Are you now or have you ever been a member of the Communist Party?"

For some the memories have faded and retain a dreamlike quality of faces, voices, and images, punctuated by sparkling opening nights and dog-eared reviews.

This book is dedicated to them, the Federal Theatre Project players, their dreams, their daring, and their still-burning commitment to the American theatre. And the rest is history. . . .

Bonnie Nelson Schwartz
December 2002

"FREE, ADULT, AND UNCENSORED"

From the first use of projections, sound, and mixed media on the American stage to the breaking of stereotypes for black actors and playwrights in a deeply segregated nation, the Federal Theatre Project broke new ground, bringing theatre to people in every corner of the nation. Its innovations, contributions, and challenges to the American theatre were enormous. In the words of Harry Hopkins, its creator, it was "free, adult, and uncensored."

The Federal Theatre performed in parks and on showboats, in circus tents and schools, in Broadway theatres and community centers. It very nearly became the first American national theatre. It popularized the socially relevant themes of Sinclair Lewis, Clifford Odets, Elmer Rice, and many others. Then it all came to an end—killed in a firestorm of controversy.

Voices from the Federal Theatre features survivors, the men and women of the 1930s' Federal Theatre Project who lived the story. In never-before-published interviews, they speak out on the controversial stories, events, and productions of the Federal Theatre Project.

As with any history, it is the personal stories—the people who were there—that grip us. Interviews with Federal Theatre actors, directors, designers, producers, and dancers—such as Arthur Miller, Studs Terkel, Jules Dassin, Katherine Dunham, Rosetta LeNoire, John Houseman, and many others—describe a vibrant, colorful, politically explosive time when the seeds were sown for what would become the controversial role of government in American art and culture.

Rare archival photographs of rehearsal and production, costume and set designs, letters and diaries, reviews, and private and publicity stills document the personal stories. Sealed away for nearly thirty years and nearly destroyed, they were rescued by Dr. Lorraine Brown of George Mason University and John O'Connor of the Library of Congress.

VOICES FROM THE
FEDERAL THEATRE

THE
ACTORS

PERRY BRUSKIN

CHILDREN'S THEATRE UNIT, NEW YORK

Here I was a rear end of a horse being cheered by kids. What else can you take with you for life? It was beautiful.

We were called the Theatre of Action, but we were from the Workers' Laboratory Theatre, which had been a real agitprop worker's theatre. We just didn't do theatre; we did Theatre! We did what we had to do.

Here was a new kind of theatre that was being focused and directed toward working people, working people who didn't even go to the theatre with a capital T, because you had to belong to the middle class to afford it. Instead, the theatre was going to the people. It was, forgive the expression, a revolutionary concept.

We lived together. It was an exciting time in our lives. We were making a kind of historical theatrical statement when we caught the attention of Hallie Flanagan. Elia Kazan[1] was our director. You'll see that he never mentions it in anything he ever says or does. One of the reasons, I think, is because it was a flop. It was not the best directorial thing he had ever done, nor was it the best play we had ever done.

We ran, I think, six weeks, when we were notified that the Federal Theatre would be interested in us, even when our show was closing. All we had to do was to prove that we didn't have any money or food. That was an easy thing in those days. They put us on relief. As professional actors, of course, we were all members of Equity already.

We could apply as professionals for Federal Theatre. I must tell you that Federal Theatre seemed to be very pleased to get us, all of our bodies. We had developed a reputation as being a rowdy, noisy, aggressive bunch. We were gonna bring excitement into the life of the Federal Theatre.

UNION PROBLEMS

There were enormous battles in Actors' Equity Association at that time. I remember those battles. In one of our meetings, at the Hotel Astor, there was this large auditorium where we would meet once every six months. The rigidity of the battle lines were drawn just as strongly there as anyplace else in the country. The left-wingers would try to mingle there, and right-wingers would try to mingle there.

One day at one of the meetings, Gilmore—who was a very elderly man, the original president of the union—got up and tried to speak. He was shouted down by the left-wingers in the audience. There was a big elephant of a man in the back trying to get the floor. The president was deliberately avoiding him and going on with the business of the meeting. We said, "Let him talk. Let him talk." This was columnist Heywood Broun.[2] He lumbered all the way up to the stage, got to the microphone, and said, "Fellow workers—" and the place came apart, because "fellow workers" was a cry that only left-wingers would use. You don't say "fellow workers" to an actors' group. These are artists. These are not working people. The battle raged on.

For most of the unions, the Federal Theatre was a serious threat to their stability as an organization, because they had indeed set up contracts in their fields, and all of the terms had been decided on. All of a sudden comes the Federal Theatre, which doesn't recognize this. We were getting twenty-three dollars and eighty-six cents a week. That was not a union salary. How does a union conform to that? Equity was not left-wing oriented. It did not have the kind of representation in the union that would say we're sympathetic with what Federal Theatre is doing.

Within Equity there were very few black actors. There was a conservative, reactionary body within Equity, and it was a solid unit, keeping blacks out of Equity or keeping them in only certain theatres, trying not to mix. If you would accept them, greet them at a union meeting, you were clearly the other side. You were clearly a Communist.

By the same token, there was a solid unit of progressive people in Equity. If you gave us swords and helmets, we would fight it out left and right, and we would all be bloodied at the end of the battle. The Negro performer was a very vital part of the left-wing position. We did everything possible in presenting *Black Pit* and *Stevedore*,[3] which got more support from the progressive community in New York than almost any other plays. Both plays were powerful, and they in effect demonstrated the kind of feeling both within Equity and within the city itself. There was a sense of excitement about a black performer being recognized. It had never been done before. This was all new.

We were lefties. We sneered at what they did on Broadway. Musicals were done for the tired businessman. Entertainment is what they were looking for. They certainly weren't gonna do *Black Pit* on Broadway. That's why the Group Theatre[4] was so important in that period. The Group Theatre kept reminding Broadway that there was something else to think about.

THE GOLDEN AGE OF SECOND AVENUE

The Yiddish theatre of that period was one of the most dynamic live theatre production units in the country. Second Avenue was Jewish Broadway, and I say it with delight. I say it with kind of a reminiscent joy because you had the Yiddish theatre family, Thomaschevsky, the great Adler. The stories are so beautiful and so touching about that period and those people. They would tour Jewish communities all over the country, and they would bring in real classics in Yiddish. Jules Dassin and I did a thing called *Marriage Proposal* by Chekhov, and we traveled together. There were magnificent Jewish writers and poets.

THE CHILDREN'S THEATRE UNIT

Some of us went into the Experimental Theatre Unit. I was sent to the Children's Theatre because they were replacing one of the guys in *The Emperor's New Clothes*. Jules Dassin was playing Zan. I was called in to replace a man by the name of Sam Bonnell. Both of these young men had been close to our theatre, though never members of it. Everybody in the kind of worker's movement of theatre at that time had respect and awe and anger at the Worker's Laboratory Theatre. *The Emperor's New Clothes* turned out to be a marvelously exciting part of Federal Theatre which I will never forget. It got very good reviews, and we played everywhere. Now, when I say "everywhere," I mean almost literally. We used to take *The Emperor's New Clothes*, with these marvelous costumes, really beautifully directed and beautifully staged, and we played the parks.

These enormous moving-van trucks would move into the center of a park. The side of the truck would come down and become the stage floor, with little ramps or pulleys holding it up, and we would do the play. It was such a marvelous kind of theatre, the Federal Children's Theatre. As big as the park was, that's how many children there were.

Whenever you played in the park, there was no admission. To this day I have never seen that many groups of children in the park. There seemed to be thousands of children.

One of the shows we did was called *Horse Play*. I was the rear end of the horse. The reason I played the rear end of the horse is that I was short. I could lift the front end of the horse so that he could paw the air, and the children would writhe and scream. I remember the front end of the horse—the guy's name was Vito, a young fellow. When we got close to the kids, they were pretending to be afraid of the horse or whatever, you know. In the horse's skin is a little stomach net facing down for me to breathe, and at the same time I could look out. While I was walking, I could only see the ground, but when the time came for me to lift the front of the horse, I could see the kids. Here I was a rear end of a horse being cheered by kids. What else can you take with you for life? It was beautiful.

REVOLT OF THE BEAVERS

Revolt of the Beavers[5] is the climax of the history of the Federal Theatre. It was the beginning of the end. Interestingly enough, though this production was done as a Children's Theatre production, it played in a Broadway theatre, the Adelphi. It was under the Children's Theatre heading, but the directors and the actors were from different areas of the Federal Theatre. How and why it came together I don't know.

Two of the writers were people who had been developed at the Workers' Laboratory Theatre. Oscar Saul, who later in life became a film producer in California, and Lou Lantz, his cowriter, got together. Here we were all together. All kinds of things that I had never seen before in Federal Theatre began to happen.

It was a play with music. They must have felt very certain that this was a very good play, because it stayed in the theatre where we were rehearsing it on Broadway. It was a simple little story of poor, little beavers who overcame the fat, rich beaver. When you put that in front of kids, that's all it was. Put that in front of an adult audience, it became a sophisticated, dramatic, Communist plot to overthrow the rich.

Skating beavers were all part of the working class beavers. That play, if it had played for the audience for whom it was intended, would not have been the one that is called the end of the Federal Theatre. Put this play in front of a mature audience looking for mature reasons and ideas, it becomes a radical look at the rich against the poor. There was this lovely little song, which I never got to sing because I was just a skating beaver [sings]:

> My favorite instrument is the fife; I tiddle-iddle, iddle-dee;
> I'm also fond of the fiddle; I tiddle-iddle, iddle-dee;
> I sit on the left, and I sit on the right,
> But my favorite spot is the middle.
>
> Oh, I was out in the woods one day, and the sights were fair to see,
> And on this side was a gay array of sights so fair to see;
> Oh, the side on the right was lovely, too, and there I would have stood,
> But the sight on the left was lovely, too, so I sit right here instead.
> Here I sit, here I sit with a heart as heavy as lead;
> I could only see one, so I didn't see none;
> Give me eyes in the back of my head;
> It's a pity, it's a pity, it's a marvelous, wonderful shame;
> It's a pity, it's a pity, and I don't know whom to blame.

Now the question is, How come I remember that song? You know how many years ago this was, and I never forgot it.

The Weapon That Destroyed the Federal Theatre

Revolt of the Beavers became known as the weapon that destroyed the Federal Theatre. I certainly know they used it as a weapon in Congress because it said, in effect, that the rich people have all the power, and the poor people should take that power away from them. We could see the children lining up in the streets with guns and going out in revolt. Oh, there were children in the audience, and there were just a lot of adults there, as well, so that it couldn't just be called a children's play.

PLAYING HAMLET IN EVERY HAMLET

I had reached the point in my life where I could afford to live in a little room, part of a larger apartment with two other theatre people. This was down in the Village on Hudson Street. That was a new world for me. I was happy to have found a status as an actor. I was respected. I got calls for many different parts. They wanted me to play in Shakespeare's *Coriolanus*. They wanted me to play in Children's Theatre, and I felt pleased and proud.

Then came the warning that Federal Theatre was on its way out, and I'll never forget. We still came to sign in and still made wisecracks, but as you can readily suspect, those wisecracks had a different note about them, a different quality in their sound. Don't forget that we had experienced the validity and the positive cultural and humanitarian value of this Federal Theatre. I can't remember the name of this marvelous actor who said he had played Hamlet in every hamlet in the Midwest. He was from the Chicago unit. I remember the people from the various units coming together and trying to be very bravado about the whole thing. The whole concept of the government giving work to people who wanted to work and could and did turned out to be such a positive thing. I guess it hit me pretty deep.

The fact is that this summer stock producer got me just at the time Federal Theatre was closing. So I went from Federal Theatre to summer stock, and you know what the first play we did was? *The Cradle Will Rock*.

If you hear silence, listen to it very closely, because it can be so many things. It has already been so many things. I can be pretentious and say theatre is as old as life. The storytellers in the beginning in the caves and around the fireplace—that was theatre.

PERRY BRUSKIN *went on to become a stage manager and the director of award-winning New York plays, including* The Hostage, The Lark, *and* Two's Company. *He still maintains an office at 1720 Broadway in the Ed Sullivan Theatre building.*

JEFF COREY

FEDERAL THEATRE, NEW YORK

*I remember these guys trying to shave with the saltwater of the East River.
It was an abysmal time. So many guys never went back to their families.
So many kids didn't know who Papa was.*

1930, the country was broke. I won a scholarship at the Fagan School of Dramatic Art, and I remember walking to the school on West 58th Street above Broadway. Roosevelt had closed the banks that particular day.

Usually, my parents gave me a quarter every day—ten cents for car fare, fifteen cents to get some food at the automat around the corner. I loved acting at the Fagan School. There were performances, and it was pretty damn thrilling. In the summer I worked in a factory on 15th Street above Fifth Avenue. We were making laminated signs for things I never heard of. We worked for eight dollars a week—a six-day week, straight time or overtime.

One day Roosevelt was to come down from Columbus Square to Union Square to perk up the attitude about work with the WPA. I asked the bosses, "He's coming by the corner at 3:25; can we leave our workbench and see Roosevelt?" He said, "Absolutely not." So I went back feeling defeated. Then I got my social activity dander up, and I said, "Come on, guys—let's go." We left our workbenches just in time to see Al Jolson walking in front of Roosevelt. He had the most handsome visage I've ever seen in anyone in my life. We went back to the factory, and the bosses didn't say a word. After the summer break, I went back to the Fagan School and invited all of these working stiffs to see me play Malvolio in *Twelfth Night*. I think none of them even heard of Shakespeare, but they loved it. Subsequently, they'd call me up to say, "When are you doing another play? When are you doing another play?"

In the May Day parades, trade unioners would march with civil liberty unions. We'd march down Fifth Avenue with the Socialist Party, the IWW, left-wing groups, and also the old, established mine workers' union. You just kind of got caught up with the zeal. Then there were the sit-ins at the factories. I guess most of the young people I know just felt that Roosevelt would be our savior, because we felt he was really on the left of center.

When I was through with the Fagan School, I worked with Children's Theatre. We did plays like *Aladdin* and *Robin Hood* and *Dick Whittington*. We were paid. I think it was twenty dollars a week, and we toured the country in a station wagon. It was so exciting seeing the country during the Depression. We'd come to a big city—Chicago, you know, Cincinnati, and Cleveland— and we play in real big theatres. So I did that for two years.

After that, with the Depression still lingering, I got a part as a spear-carrier in Leslie Howard's *Hamlet*. Leslie was a British matinee idol. When someone left the company, he auditioned the four spear-carriers for the part of Rosencrantz. I got it and joined Actors' Equity on the second of January 1937, and I really felt, Boy, I have a profession.

Howard was just a wonderful, irritating person. We were very close to him. He'd get into his moods where he'd be downright destructive and full of animosity, and then he could be gentle and sweet and learned. There was a small radio station doing a series of radio things—*Workers on the March.* Howard directed then, and I did a lot of those. That was the first radio work that I did. Poor Howard, he'd really get himself agitated; didn't know what the hell to do with him.

I saw the whole thing—the Dust Bowl. We traveled by train with Leslie Howard, and we'd see these freight cars come with people just moving west. I remember in New York before there was an East Side Highway [perhaps FDR Drive?], seeing all these guys from all over the country. They found fish crates and made houses from them. I remember these guys trying to shave with the saltwater of the East River. It was an abysmal time. So many guys never went back to their families. So many kids didn't know who Papa was.

I knew John Houseman because he directed Leslie Howard's *Hamlet*. Jack was a gentleman. Actually, he was born in Austria, but his family went to

England. He was very courteous, a rather benevolent man, anything but pushy. We used to call him Jack.

Orson [Welles] was like Sammy Glick—pushy, pushy, pushy. The first time I saw Orson, he and Paul Robeson had the same kind of charisma. Orson had a fine mind, and he was hooked into things. Orson had a powerful presence. I think he was really very, very gifted, but there was something in him that was destructive. It would have been wonderful if his theatre was able to be the core of a national theatre.

It was 1938, and I'd just been married. I got in the Federal Theatre because I had a good resume, and I had been a working actor for four years. I got a twenty-seven-dollar check, which was very meaningful at those times. My first assignment was to do A Marriage Proposal,[6] which is a farce of Chekhov's. Al Sachs, who was the director of the Theatre of Action, was on the WPA. He directed us in the play, and it was so good that they decided the best venue would be for us to do it in clown makeup. I still have my old makeup box, and I still cherish that white stuff. The clowns of the real circus would show us how to use clown makeup, and he did Chekhov's Marriage Proposal as a clownish farce. After that, the big deal was to do it at Washington Square Park, because we knew we'd get important people to see it.

The WPA had put up buildings. We played in some of those theatres, like in Kansas City, Missouri. There was a wonderful WPA-constructed theatre where we played in Bakersfield, California, the Biltmore Theatre.

Then I segued into a production of Life and Death of an American.[7] We rehearsed and rehearsed for about eleven months before it started. I thought that was a little demoralizing, but it all worked out. Arthur Kennedy played the lead. I was one of four narrators, and we had a lot to narrate about. We played at the Maxine Elliot Theatre, and our position was in one of the box seats talking to the audience. It turned out to be very, very successful. It included vaudeville acts, symphonic music, and war music. It was a very meaningful play written by George Sklar. It got great reviews, and Piscator, the German director who had worked with Reinhardt, said, "This is by far the greatest theatre event in ten years." He said it was really the definitive epic theatre, worthy of Bertolt Brecht.

It was kind of a boondoggling, I think. We rehearsed, probably not eleven months, but it seemed like eleven years. Let's cut it down to, say, seven months. But we were ready to do it a long time ago. The sets were wonderful. The lighting by Jean Rosenthal[8] was remarkable. It was a mixture of sequences about World War I, working-class people who had lost an arm and a leg and came back to find no job. The overall feeling about the whole play was the life and death of an American reduced to being a pauper and the effect it had on people's families.

I didn't regard it as agitprop. I'd also worked at the Theatre Collective. This is where I met Johnny Randolph. He told me, "You were the best actor there." I don't know whether I was the best actor there, but it was my first experience with the method.

I was so enamored with the Group Theatre. They'd come by, and we did scenes from *Waiting for Lefty*, and then we did a Philip Stevenson play about the American Revolution. We were doing grotesque things, so I found that rather interesting and very freeing. There were no real styles; it's your style. Brecht called it didactic theatre. You sit there and listen. We're gonna show you what your life is about or what your life should not be or what it should.

THE BEGINNING OF THE END

When the WPA was scuttled, I just couldn't find work. I had a good background, you know, touring the country and doing these plays. I told my wife that I wanted to have a life and a family, and I'm getting nowhere on Broadway, which was in very bad condition. I said, "I'm gonna go to the Brooklyn Engineering Institute and study, take a course in blueprint reading," and I went there a couple of times.

Finally, my wife said, "Listen, we got a couple of hundred dollars in the bank. Let's go to California. You always talked about it." I said, "Okay." We got our Model A Ford from an auction for seventy dollars. Gasoline, I think, must have been like eight cents a gallon, and we'd stop at motels for seventy-five cents or a dollar.

In time Hallie Flanagan was to appear before the Dies Committee, and she was questioned about her background and so forth. They wanted to know about these Red plays that they were doing. She mentioned Christopher Marlowe, and [Rep. Joe Starnes, D-AL] said, "Who is this Marlowe fellow, so we can get in touch with him?" She said, "He happens to be the greatest playwright preceding Shakespeare." Of course, everybody laughed, and then [Rep. Martin Dies, D-TX] said, "Well, it's one o'clock; we're gonna break for lunch." She said, "Will I be able to testify after lunch?" He said, "We'll see about it after lunch." There was no after lunch. That was the beginning of the end of the Federal Theatre.

Tallulah Bankhead and Raymond Massey and people of that stature, when the curtain came down, they would announce to the people, the audience, "You must join the people who are protesting the closing of the Federal Theatre in Times Square." The whole audience would walk from the theatre to Times Square. There were these mass protests, and they made you think, "We've won. We've won. We've got everything going for us. They can't cut off this promising Federal Theatre." But it went down the dumpster, and that was unfortunate.

In the case of *Life and Death of an American*, there were so many ex-vaude-villians and chorus girls and so forth who knew nothing about politics at all, who did not vote for Franklin Roosevelt. There were a lot of people who were just kind of passive reactionaries, but there were also people who you could call comrades. Perry Bruskin was a narrator, so I guess there were left-wing people doing the narrating, and one guy who was quite reactionary.

I think it was a kind of Romantic movement rather than a political move-ment. People thought, "Oh, my God. Paradise opened up." And Earl Browder, who was head of the Communist Party, said, "Communism is twentieth-century democracy." You'd see people marching on May Day and the IWW, the Socialist Party, the Communist Party, the Young Communist Organization, and it seemed so positive. In time we realized that we were all screwed up, because I think, How could I have been so naive to accept this thing? I must say, when I came to Hollywood—and a lot of the Group Theatre people were there, and they became very good friends—I'd play tennis with Kazan. Everyone was kind of left-wing. It seemed a comfortable thing to be.

We established the Actors' Lab in Los Angeles, and it was ultimately Red-baited by the California subcommittee on Communist activities, and that was the beginning of the end of the Actors' Lab. By then I don't think there were too many people who were still going to Communist Party meet-ings. The people who would go to meetings like this were prestigious and intelligent, and they'd talk about Goethe and Schiller, and at the Actors' Lab, we'd do remote plays like Pirandello. It was really a cultural hub. It was beautiful. This was the people's theatre. You know, there were full houses, and people were happy with it.

There were party affiliations that I think just withered away. It was a thing of the past, but when the House committee came by, they didn't want to hear about changes in people's attitudes.

❖   ❖   ❖

JEFF COREY *(1914–2002) began his career in the 1930s playing Shakespeare. One of his first roles was Rosencrantz in Leslie Howard's* Hamlet. *He was blacklisted in the early 1950s for refusing to name names before the House Un-American Activities Committee and didn't work as an actor again for more than a decade. He turned to teaching and established the Actors' Lab in Hollywood, where his students included James Dean, Anthony Perkins, Jane Fonda, and Jack Nicholson. Corey appeared in more than 100 feature films, including* Home of the Brave, My Friend Flicka, Joan of Arc *with Ingrid Bergman,* Butch Cassidy and the Sundance Kid, In Cold Blood, Beneath the Planet of the Apes, *and* True Grit *with John Wayne.*

JULES DASSIN

CHILDREN'S THEATRE UNIT, NEW YORK

Mother Goose is no longer a rhymed escapist. She has been studying Marx; Jack and Jill lead the class revolution.

Brooks Atkinson reviewing Revolt of the Beavers *in the* New York Times, *1937*

I was part of the Yiddish theatre, the Artef Theatre.[9] I remember that not very good work was being done on Broadway. The menu was melodramas and pleasant plays. The Yiddish theatre was doing the classics, and it was just a richer and more cultured theatre.

When the news came about the Federal Theatre, everybody ran to register. You had to go somewhere to say, "I'm an actor," and they took you at your word. I had to pass the audition. It was that simple.

It was a very exciting idea. It was born out of the time when America was going through such crises, and it was just a seemingly spontaneous, natural expression to deal with our daily lives and daily problems. Some wonderful work was done—some really wonderful work and wonderful theatre.

I was in the Children's Theatre Unit. The first show was an adaptation of *The Emperor's New Clothes*.[10] Sam Bonnell and I were the two charlatan tailors. I remember we were free to do almost anything, a lot of improvisations. One time we were angry at the behavior of an actor, and we came in with two pairs of scissors and cut his clothes off. It was that free. I still hear the great pleasure and shouts of glee and warnings by the kid audiences. That was lovely.

We did the famous *Revolt of the Beavers*, which seemingly almost destroyed the U.S. government, it was so subversive. It was about the working beavers and the fat beavers who made the poor other beavers work. We had all kinds of wonderful things onstage—mills and straps—and there was a fat beaver who exploited us. This was denounced as communist, subversive, destructive stuff. What is not known is that Elia Kazan was set to direct *Revolt of the Beavers*, and then he thought better of it. He was replaced by somebody else who was also part of the Group Theatre.

The Living Newspaper was a very interesting new form dictated more by the time than any subversive mind. Remember, we're in the thirties—bad, difficult time. It just seemed natural to everybody that instead of doing a straight play, to say, "Let's reflect what we're living here." Living, indeed. The Living Newspaper was a documentary form but usually so skillfully done—good theatre, good drama, but there was always a point. That was no more a communist idea than the whole Federal Theatre was a communist idea.

The charge that the Federal Theatre was communist-dominated is another ridiculous assumption. There were communists around. We're talking about the thirties, when many people, including me, thought that this was an idea that we had to learn and care about, because we were talking about people. We were talking about social security, about the sanctity of a trade union. Well, these are all like America and apple pie. That it was branded communist was foolish. Of course, there were communists around, as there were all kinds of beliefs and denominations. The Communist Party in America, in terms of power or size, was almost a joke. I think at their largest they were about eighty thousand members nationally. Of course, reflected in this attack was the attack on Franklin Delano Roosevelt, who realized that people had to eat and had to be given work and that the whole capitalist system was in danger, and he had to save it. I think more than 90 percent of the press was against Franklin Delano Roosevelt, and that was all a part of it.

I don't know whether it's correct to say that these people were afraid of the theatre. You know, there's a special thing in the theatre: contact. You have an audience and actor working together, and the impact is very strong. I think it's that simple. The hatred and the anger for the theatre, because people's problems were being expressed, were resented by very foolish people. Mr. Martin Dies, yes, I remember: a rather stupid man, a real philistine who had no grasp at all of what a wonderful thing was growing in the American culture. He saw the Red under every bed and under every dressing room and every backstage.

Very soon after the tragic pink-slip days when people were being fired, a very interesting man, Martin Gabel, came to me and said, "I want to do a Living Newspaper on Broadway, and I would like you to direct it." Indeed, *Medicine Show*[11] came to Broadway. It was very daring. It was a very strong criticism of the American Medical Association, their campaigns against any organized social medicine. There was a lot of factual stuff about how many places in America, not just small towns, were without hospitals, sometimes without doctors. Well, this too was considered very subversive stuff. It didn't last long. I remember Gabel finally playing in it, as well, and we discovered a new young actress whose name was Dorothy McGuire. That was my first appearance in the Broadway theatre.

The dissolution of the Federal Theatre was, to me, a severe loss ranging on criminal. I have seen theatre in many parts of the world, national theatres, but I insist today that the best national theatre in the world would have been here in the United States, growing out of the Federal Theatre. It's sad; it's grievous.

The Federal Theatre was part of a movement in America to put people to work, and this wonderful idea to put them to work in the cultural field was such a big moment for America—for education, for culture—that we still mourn its loss.

❖   ❖   ❖

JULES DASSIN *has been called "a man of mystery." Few know that he was born in America and later exiled to Europe by the Hollywood Blacklist. Beginning his career in the 1930s in New York's Yiddish theatre, he became a member of the Federal Theatre's Children's Unit. An internationally respected actor, director, and writer, he directed such films as* Never on Sunday, *in which he costarred with his wife, Melina Mercouri, and* Rififi, Topkapi, Phaedra, *and* The Naked City. *He is presently living in Greece, where he oversees the Melina Mercouri Foundation.*

ROSETTA LeNOIRE
NEGRO THEATRE UNIT, NEW YORK

I remember so many fights in the lobby about having people of black skin play Shakespeare. Oh, they were really bad. They didn't want us to play it. If it was a maid's role, go ahead, but if it was something from the classics, no.

I grew up against the background of racism in the United States. It's hard for me to believe, yet I know: I lived it. Discrimination, especially in New York, was terrible, just awful.

I come from a mixed family. Grandpa Burton was white. He was pure-white Englishman from a financially substance family. He used to call me his little chocolate drop. In Dominica, the French West Indies, they don't give a darn about your color. If they fall in love, they fall in love, and they go ahead and have twenty children, you know [laughs]. I grew up in that.

GROWING UP IN HELL'S KITCHEN

I grew up on Forty-ninth Street between Ninth and Tenth Avenues, which was known to all as Hell's Kitchen. It wasn't easy in those days. I still remember it. I used to get beaten up because I was colored.

I'll never forget that as a little girl seven years of age, I saw my mother die . . . because they would not take her in Harlem Hospital when she was

giving birth. Those days most women, white and colored, had their children
at home, and they didn't have any professional help. They gave birth like
their grandmothers did. My mother was carrying my youngest brother. She
got started with the pains of birth. They took her to this hospital downtown,
where they said, "Take her up to Harlem." They took her straight up to
Harlem. When they got to Harlem Hospital, [people there] said, "Throw the
nigger out," and they pushed her out the door, and [she] fell on the steps and
died. I will never forget it, never, never.

First of all, I couldn't walk because I had rickets. In those days the medical society was still doing a hell of a lot of research on children that were
born 'cause there were so many children born in those days with rickets. My
legs were operated on by so very many times by various doctors. As a little, bitty
baby girl, I was funny as all get out and being funny and people smiling at me
all the time; I would just continue to work harder to get them to keep on
smiling.

That's where the whole thing started, even with the broken legs, learning
to dance and the rhythm. Uncle Bo [Bill "Bojangles" Robinson][12] was like
that, too. I started calling him Uncle Bo, especially after my mother died; he
became a friend. Up until he became a big star, he used to sleep in the subway, under the stairs. He didn't have anything. He never dreamed that he was
gonna become a star; that was the furthest thing from his mind. He treated
me as though I was his child. He really adored me. He's the one that nick-
named me Brown Sugar.

I worked for years playing every role that was ever written for a maid
[laughs]. Then I began to get better roles in the Federal Theatre. They were
always calling: "Get Brown Sugar; she can play it."

One thing you did, you applied for relief, especially if your mother and
your father both are not working. Then you had to prove that you had, at
some time in life, been in a play or a musical or sang in the church choir, and
then you'd give the church choir or the director's name and telephone number. They would send you a script, and you would get it about a week ahead,
and you would have to memorize it. The scripts were not as wonderful as they
are now. Then they'd call you and have you come down and audition for the
musical director, the choreographer, and all.

I'll never forget: My father must have said to one of his friends, "I have a
daughter who is very talented, and Bill 'Bojangles' Robinson taught her to tap

dance." "Yeah? What's her name?" The next thing you know, I would get a telephone call or a card saying they want me to come to such and such a theatre.

THE NEGRO THEATRE UNIT IN HARLEM

I was in the *"Voodoo" Macbeth*. I played one of the witches. I remember we had to have some sort of long pants with rows of frills at the bottom, and a lot of fur. Of course, they had a lot of wigs that we had to wear, white, black, green, or yellow.

I remember so many fights in the lobby about having people of black skin play Shakespeare. Oh, they were really bad. They didn't want us to play it. If it was a maid's role, go ahead, but if it was something from the classics, no.

The *Voodoo Macbeth* was at the old Lafayette Theatre. Lord, have mercy. Whew! At theatre time you couldn't walk by. There was no place for you to walk—especially when they had intermission and people came out. There were those who just raved about it, and there were those that tried to tear it down, but it ran forever, and they came from everywhere. They even came from Europe to see it. If you bought a year ahead, you still couldn't get tickets.

It was the Federal Theatre that gave us so many of our great actors, because they were permitted to play roles that they would have never been offered on Broadway. It gave us our Canada Lee.[13] Canada Lee was wonderful in *Macbeth*. He was terrific. Everybody respected him and looked up to him.

It was very difficult because people didn't have the money to have the big musicals, and that's where, if you were black, you would certainly end up in the chorus. The audiences adored the choruses. When you would bring in a whole chorus of black actors to dance for just one number, they would stand, they would scream.

They'd come back to see that show two and three times. They were familiar with the music, because they bought the record and would get in the aisles and dance. You'd have two shows, one on the stage and one on the aisles. And you would run forever.

A lot of white authors started writing roles for black or tan people without the heavy Southern accent, and those shows cleaned up financially. It only goes to prove to you, all of us like to see positive things on stage.

Orson Welles was something else, I'm telling you. A lot of women of all ages considered him their father, of every race, color, or creed. Mr. Welles would raise hell if anybody was in the least nasty to me or tried to ignore me or tried to confuse me.

Mr. Houseman—there were times when the colored people had to protect him; he was so good and so nice to everybody. We all felt that he was our personal father or uncle or cousin or brother.

Orson was still young. He was born a genius on every level. Not just I, but everyone who has ever worked with him—right now tears are coming to my eyes because there was something so special about that man. I will never forget: One of the actors said, "When I die, if I go to heaven and he's not there, if Orson isn't there, I'm gonna picket" [laughs], and we all fell out in the floor laughing 'cause that was so funny. But that's how much we all loved him, every race, color, and creed.

Orson would now and then say, "Let's take that scene over again—the scene that we did about an hour and a half ago. Like if it was your uncle or your father, what would you do if you were having the same problem or same discussion? How would you talk to him?" He had the best attitude when directing. He would say, "Listen, Sugar; hey, honeybun"—always started out with something to weaken you inside, warm and lovely. Then he'd say, "Listen, hon, you know what you just said, and you know the way you said it? Were you angry? Well, that line, it's not an angry line, is it? Well, how would you say that if you were saying that from your heart to somebody that you loved?" Or "How would you say it to somebody you couldn't stand?" He would help you to really get the feeling of what would be going on inside of you.

He was wonderful. He was pure heaven, pure heaven. I used to say, "You know one thing: I hope when the time come for me to meet Orson or some of the other players that were there, I hope that we can be together and do things this way." Then you'd say, "Hey, Orson. Remember that line that I couldn't get right whatnot? Would we say it that way today, or would we say it in another way?" [laughs] And he would start laughing like crazy and say, "You're always looking to make some trouble, aren't you?"

When Houseman and Welles left, everything changed. To me it was though you had put the mixture of a wonderful cake in the oven and started to bake, and then all of a sudden it was as though you forgot to put the baking powder in, because it fell; the whole thing fell.

The Federal Theatre gave you, me, and everybody else an opportunity for a larger education on many levels. It enlightened you to the background of every nationality. There is something wonderful about it. It made me open my mind.

AMAS

I founded a company, the Amas, "you love." I founded that because I was coming from a mixed family. I got sick and tired of the discrimination business, so that's why I founded Amas. Oh God, the kind of reviews we received. We had to open our theatre an hour ahead of time.

It was so difficult at the time, too. I would do housework in the morning for people, Jewish people and Irish people, and that helped me to get the money to start this little off-Broadway theatre.

❖   ❖   ❖

ROSETTA LeNOIRE'S *career began in the Federal Theatre. Bill* "Bojangles" Robinson *was her godfather, and Eubie Blake her mentor. Miss LeNoire made her Broadway debut in 1939 in Mike Todd's* Hot Mikado, *appearing in such plays as* Blues for Mr. Charlie, Lost in the Stars, The Sunshine Boys, *and* You Can't Take It with You. *She had a flourishing career well into her 70s and 80s and appeared regularly in such television hits as* Family Matters, Amen, *and* Give Me a Break.

NORMAN LLOYD

LIVING NEWSPAPER UNIT, NEW YORK

When we had scenes in the Living Newspaper which touched a nerve, or a personality who offended them, they would talk back to the actor on the stage, because they'd never been in a live theatre, and maybe that's what you did. That's dangerous from a certain point of view.

Joe Losey[14] got me involved. He was a director on the Federal Theatre Project. He later turned out to be one of my most talented film directors, but at this point Joe was going to direct a project called the Living Newspaper in a Broadway theatre. I had worked with Joe Losey before in the theatre, and he wanted someone who could carry these sketches. He was not happy with the talent he had at the time, so he got permission to go outside the relief project and get an actor who was looking for a job—in this case myself. So that's how I got on the Federal Theatre.

My first show was called *Triple-A Plowed Under*.[15] It was the story of the farmer's desperate plight in the Depression, including the Dust Bowl. I did a number of quick scenes in it. They were almost like sketches. You would go from one to another. In one I'd wear a suit. In another I changed character and wore a cap, and I was a worker in that. In *Injunction Granted*, I ended up as Justice Brandeis in a robe. It was the last shot, as I recall, against a projection of the Preamble of the Constitution: "We the people" and so forth. There were these four figures in silhouette: Justice Brandeis; Al Smith; Earl Browder, leader of the Communist Party at that time; and one other person.

The audience would boo and hiss and catcall and all sorts of things. As a consequence of this, the actor who was getting twenty-three dollars and eighty-seven cents a week believed that he was the star of the show because he got this response from the audience

THE LIVING NEWSPAPER

A living newspaper was a concept. My first knowledge of it comes from Piscator, who was a European director and who worked with Brecht. They had what they called Epic theatre, a theatre that was antinaturalistic and more expressionistic. You use film and you use projections. It was quite stylized. Its purpose was a learning kind of theatre, so to speak. It was brought to this country first by Hallie Flanagan for her theatre at Vassar, where she did a living newspaper called $E = mc^2$.

Its great development was on the Federal Theatre. This largely came about because of Heywood Broun. Heywood Broun was one of the leading newspaper writers in America. He had been a sports columnist, and his work was the best of the period of newspaper writing. He was stagestruck. He had during the Depression done a review called *Shoot the Works*. He felt that with the Federal Theatre doing plays for all sorts of people—the classical theatre, the Yiddish theatre, the opera, dance—there was nothing being done for the newspaperman. He got this idea of a newspaper with a city room and all the guys at the desks. These guys were led by a writer named Arthur Arent.[16] They did something that television does now: change the programs every day as the news changed.

Triple-A Plowed Under was only forty-five minutes long. We used to do two a night. All changed, and we dropped all the latest news projections, but it had all these elements I've described—of film, projections, music, choreography—dealing with issues of the day, of the moment.

Losey gave me the script, and there was nothing I wanted to do in it, but I had an idea that it needed some kind of comic alleviation. It was rather didactic. It was the history of labor in the courts. That's hardly something to bring an audience in, and I thought it needed something to jazz it up. Just at that time the Barnum and Bailey Circus came into New York. They used to play Madison Square Garden and then would go out to the other end of Brooklyn. They used to play under a tent there, and I wanted to see the circus, not in the Garden but under a tent.

As I watched the circus, I thought, "My goodness, these clowns. Here's a wonderful thing, to take this theatrical device, so to speak, and apply it to this dry, didactic script." And Joe went with the idea. They built a whole area in the set that I could pop out of with a trapdoor. In it I kept magic tricks, which I used in the scene, a little piano, which I would play.

Virgil Thomson[17] did the score. I met him on the Sixth Avenue bus, and I said, "Oh, Virgil, you know I'm going to use a little baby's piano, and are you going to write a tune that will identify the clown?" Virgil, who had a rather penetrating voice, said, "No, dear boy, I'm going to write 'T T T' on the score." I said, "Well, what is that?" He said, "'Tunes take time'" [laughs]. So he never wrote, but he was very insistent that I do the proper fingering on this baby piano. He was a great character, and I did several shows with him.

I would make comments on everything they were doing. I had a big cigar. You know, when the guy would say something of an industrial nature, I'd pop up with a big cigar, pop down again. Then someone would make a thing about education, and I'm sitting there with a Phi Beta Kappa key that was enormous; and so on. Virgil wrote a score that consisted of ratchets, sirens, drums, ships' bells, and trombones and trumpets.

So when it all went off at one time the first night, the police burst into the theatre. They didn't know what was going on. They'd never heard such a thing coming out of there.

Injunction Granted[18] was about the history of labor in the courts. They used projections in our shows. In *Injunction Granted* they were found to be missing or mislaid and so on. There was a kind of sabotage going on because the show was favorable to labor. We knew we were doing the history of labor in the courts, but many of the actors didn't know, didn't care; it was a check.

There were some actors who were very old, who were of another time entirely. There was an actor named Wilford Clark, and he was a grand-nephew of Edwin Booth. Those men just desperately needed a check.

Morris Watson[19] had been with the Associated Press. He had had very distinguished service in World War I and had suffered some gas attacks during that war, I believe. He was a gentle man, always with a wonderful smile and absolutely one hundred percent behind what Arent and Losey were doing. He was the administrator of the Living Newspaper.

I remember a meeting in the Manhattan Opera House of the unions involved in the Federal Theatre. It was chaired by the head of the stagehands' union. Morris Watson got up to speak, and the head of the stagehands' union, with his enormous gavel pounding, said, "Meeting's over."

I remember Broun, who was out in the bar at the Manhattan Opera House, coming in and forming a phalanx as he pushed up to the stage, and I hear it to this day: "I demand this man be given the right to speak."

One of the building service employees who were involved with the stage-hands' union panicked as he got pushed out of the way and pulled a gun. Broun, totally unfazed, went on: "I demand he speak." And Morris then spoke.

Sam Jaffe was a member of the council, and he was impassioned in our defense. Sam was a well-known movie actor. Later he became famous as Doctor Zorba [on TV's *Ben Casey*] and Gunga Din [in the movie of the same name] and the Lama in *Lost Horizons*. It was a time of real union ferment and the building of those unions.

I think the best notice I've ever received as an actor was from Consolidated Edison. This was *Power*,[20] where I played Angus K. Buttoncooper. We were able to secure an interoffice memorandum that said, "The part of the consumer is played by a very clever actor who makes out a very bad case for the consumer by questioning what a watt is." That was the best notice I've ever received [laughs].

Power was basically about the TVA, the Tennessee Valley Authority, and the fight of the farmers and the people who lived in that authority to get power, which the utilities company would not give them, and the price was prohibitive. When the government came in and built the dam and gave them power, this was one of the major things in the whole Roosevelt administration. We showed how the farmers took to guns because they sensed something was going on. They'd go out, and there was Consolidated Southern, without any permission, stringing lines to put power in. Now, the government was gonna beat 'em in, and they wanted to beat the government. Farmers went out with guns and said, "Get down off that tree, because you're gonna get a bullet if you don't." They defended the government, the TVA, and got their power.

Angus K. Buttoncooper reappears in *One-Third of a Nation*.[21] Howard Bay,[22] one of our leading designers at the time, did the set, which was actually a projection about housing. Angus K. Buttoncooper was the quintessential consumer. The first scene was a very typical Living Newspaper scene. I'm in the follow spot. I'm going shopping. I want some tomatoes, and they say whatever it was a pound. I say, "Oh, no, too expensive." I go to another place, and it's less, so I say, "Give me a pound."

Then I have to pay my electric bill, and I have no place to go for a less expensive rate. There's a disembodied voice—it was the voice of the Living Newspaper in all the shows—would come through. I would talk to it, and I'd say, "It says here so much for a watt. What is a watt?" I'd get this double-talk answer. He had no place to go. They made the point with the tomatoes, you see. That was simple but effective.

ORSON WELLES AND JOHN HOUSEMAN

One cannot speak of the Federal Theatre without thinking of John Houseman and Orson Welles. John Houseman later became one of my dearest friends—my wife's and mine. These were two of the most remarkable people that I met in the theatre.

Orson's talent was of an extreme theatricality. What he brought to the American theatre, in the Federal Theatre—starting with the *"Black"* [*"Voodoo"*] *Macbeth*, set in 1814 in Haiti under the regime of [Toussaint-Louverture], and with Faustus and with *Horse Eats Hat*,[23] and of course *The Cradle Will Rock*—was a totality of theatre, which had not been seen in America by an American director. American directors were very good stagers. They could stage a play very well, like George Kaufman or George M. Cohan, but what Orson brought was a totality—the sound, the lighting, the music, and the overwhelming sense of being enveloped in a production as audience.

Houseman was, if you will, the Diaghilev of the Diaghilev-Nijinsky relationship. He could make things happen. He was a great entrepreneur. If you had an idea, he made it happen. He had in his lifetime seven separate theatre companies. You had this kind of mad organizational fellow, Houseman, who had also been in the grain business and I think arrived in the theatre because it was a depression. He didn't know what else to do. As luck would have it, he had an enormous talent to be a theatre manager and a theatre producer. The functioning of the two was brilliant, violent, and a great thing for the theatre.

Horse Eats Hat was a French farce by Labiche. It was done as a movie by Rene Claire, calling it *The Italian Straw Hat*, about a hat that has many adventures. It had great flavor, great music done by Paul Bowles, who, in the time that I knew Paul, was a prominent theatre musician.

What [Welles] brought was a brilliance of staging. Pipes would be float-
ing up and down, and Joe Cotten would get enmeshed with a pipe that would
hang a drape and find himself going up into the flys. There was a marvelous
fake horse that Bil Baird, the puppeteer, was the front legs—or was it the hind
legs?—of a very expressive horse. He cast Joe Cotten and Arlene Francis. It
was the first time I'd ever seen Joe, and I remember predicting, "This guy's
going to be a star." He had such a lovely, romantic, gentle, humorous quality,
which later paid off in some of the finest performances I've ever seen in pictures: *Citizen Kane*, *The Third Man*. Orson had great wit in the staging, very
colorful and brilliant. He brought that quality over later to the Mercury
Theatre when we did *Shoemaker's Holiday*.

Faustus was just brilliant. Orson was a magician, and he loved to be
magic. *Faustus* gave him that opportunity. You had trapdoors, lights, and people appearing, disappearing.

Orson always used all the elements that existed: sound, music, film; the
lighting of the time influenced very much by Abe Feder. Those things stimulated him, and he used them.

You had smoke; you had all the things a magician would use to mystify
you. He had a marvelous black actor named Jack Carter, who played
Mephistopheles, and he was great. It was theatricality at its best. You saw all
the elements of theatre coming together in a way that thrilled you as you sat
there in the audience.

Houseman was the old man; he was in his early thirties—different generation. Houseman was the most modern-minded fellow. He was really brilliant
in his likes and dislikes. Orson was about twenty-one. I was twenty-one. We
were all young and of course wild. We would do anything in the theatre, and
so it paid off, so to speak, in the productions.

Now, they did have a falling out eventually, and there was a period they
didn't see each other. Somehow they met in a restaurant after John had done
Julius Caesar at MGM, and Orson felt that John had stolen his play [laughs].
I was in the original production of *Julius Caesar*; that's when Orson threw the
can of Sterno at him in the restaurant, saying, "You've stolen my play!" And
John said, "*Your* play?" And they were off.

Orson was a great one for loud screaming. He was a great one for never
seeming to sleep while actors were falling down, practically. We later found
out he secretly would take naps in a hotel nearby. He also would be given to

eating at rehearsals with no one being permitted to have any food. This would get us very angry. The hunger alone would get you angry.

We were rehearsing one day, and Orson was doing his typical thing. The apron of the Mercury stage was very low, so that he could sit in the first row and eat off the apron. He'd send out to have a steak brought in and all sorts of things that go with it. He'd eat there, while we were near the verge of starvation physically, and Orson, he's just eating away. Finally, a strawberry tart was brought in with the steak. Marion Waring Manly, who was a voracious eater, couldn't take this visual thing anymore of seeing steak and strawberry tart—desperate. So she stepped downstage with Orson eating away, and she said, "Orson, please give me one strawberry. Please, Orson." That was characteristic.

In a screenplay he's written, Orson describes Marc Blitzstein coming back to meet him the first time during *Faustus*. Somehow Marc gets past the stage doorman and gets involved in all the smoke and trapdoors and lights going on—doesn't know where he is. It's a most brilliant concept. He's coming in to get him interested in something he's written called *The Cradle Will Rock*. Orson could have been the only person to shoot this, which was his memory of a time on the Federal Theatre.

HARRY HOPKINS

I remember a crowd of people, and here's Harry Hopkins. I must have met Hallie, because she was the one who made a personal request for me to go into *Sing for Your Supper*[24]—1938, wasn't it? She felt that I might make a contribution as an actor, doing the sketches and the song and dance or two, to which I agreed and did go into rehearsal. It was the show that produced the "Ballad for Americans,"[25] amongst other things. Harold Hecht was the producer.

I went into rehearsal, and at the same time I received an offer from George S. Kaufman and Max Gordon, who was one of the premier producers on Broadway, to go into a review they were doing by Harold Rome called *Sing Out the News*. They were offering me two hundred and fifty dollars a week, which was a considerable sum of money, considering that I was getting twenty-three dollars and eighty-seven cents, but I had promised Hallie I would do the show. I turned them down, because I couldn't think of myself saying to Hallie, "Well, I said I would do it, but, you know, I got more money over there, and I'm going over there." So I turned them down.

Max Gordon, the producer of the show, meets Harry Hopkins at the racetrack in Laurel, Maryland. He said, "What are you running over there?" Hop said, "What are you talking about?"

He said, "Well, I offered Norman Lloyd a part in *Sing Out the News*, and he turned me down to stay in *Sing for Your Supper* on the Federal Theatre." Hopkins said, "Oh, don't you know, that's what we do: Tax, tax, spend, spend, elect, elect." He went right back to his office after the last race, sent a wire to Hallie, said, "Fire him." And she very apologetically had to let me go. Now I had no job.

Well, the Federal Theatre and its work was what you might call liberal. They did that production of Sinclair Lewis's book *It Can't Happen Here*, which imagined what would happen if fascism came to America. Correct me if I'm wrong: Thirty-nine [twenty-five] productions opened at the same time. There were people who felt this was dangerous, I guess.

Interestingly enough, for the Living Newspaper the top [admission charge] was eighty-five cents, I believe. As a consequence, people came to the theatre who had never seen live performances before. When we had scenes in the Living Newspaper which touched a nerve, or a personality who offended them, they would talk back to the actor on the stage, because they'd never been in a live theatre, and maybe that's what you did. That's dangerous from a certain point of view. That's why you had a living, exciting social theatre in the thirties.

Today they can't afford it. As a consequence, there are fewer writers who write for the theatre. As a consequence, actors don't act in the theatre; they come out right away for television and never learn to act.

I think there was a kind of shame attached to being on the WPA, that you couldn't make it in the commercial Broadway theatre. We were too young to realize that. We just saw there was a stage and you could fill it and raise hell on it and get audiences. And that's what we did. Orson Welles and John Houseman saw it as an opportunity, as an enormous step in their career. It was a chance to do a new form that I knew nothing about. Creatively, aesthetically, it was one of the glorious opportunities of my lifetime, and one has an instinct for those things, you know, when they come along.

We almost came to greatness and just fell short. It was attacked politically. They were attacking everything, even the painting, the murals, and so
on. I . . . I think it's sad that it never happened.

❖   ❖   ❖

NORMAN LLOYD *(b. 1914) began acting with Eva Le Gallienne's Civic Repertory in New York. After the Federal Theatre Project, he joined the original company of the Orson Welles–John Houseman Mercury Theatre in 1938. He was brought to Hollywood by director Alfred Hitchcock to do the title role in 1942's* Saboteur *and went on to direct TV's long-running* Alfred Hitchcock Presents. *He became a production associate for Jean Renoir* (The Southerner) *and Charlie Chaplin* (Limelight). *Lloyd went on to direct and act in numerous television programs and films, including* St. Elsewhere, Spellbound, The Green Years, Dead Poets Society, *and* The Age of Innocence.

ALAN PETERS

TOURING FEDERAL THEATRE, CHICAGO

O say, can you sing, dance, or act?
If you can, it's a well-established fact
That Uncle Sam will take you and make you
And break you into anything.

DEPRESSION-ERA CHICAGO

I had hitchhiked across the country, and I couldn't get a job anywhere. I will tell you that the feeling was that there would be a nonpolitical revolution. The people were up to here. I mean up to here.

I spent time in hobo camps. I washed dishes. I washed windows. I shot pool. I went across the Salt Lake Desert on a freight train hanging on. It was colder than hell. How I did that one, I'll never remember. I got to Oakland. I had five cents to my name, and I got on a trolley. There was only one person I knew on the West Coast. That was Morey Amsterdam. Morey was a buddy of mine here in Chicago. There's a sign at Loew's Warfield Theatre, and I said, "Oh my God, that's where Morey is." I went backstage, and the doorman said, "I'm sorry; they're gonna go on." I said, "Just tell him Al Peters is here." Morey comes running out. The Harris Band was playing there; that became Phil Harris. I was the second banana to Morey that night.

I'll tell you, though, as I reflect upon that time, we were all trying just to get something to eat and sleep somewhere—the complete lack of any ability to get an income, to get work. Farmers, you know . . . *Triple-A Plowed Under* was not dreamed up out of the clouds. It really happened.

THE CHICAGO REPERTORY GROUP

The Chicago Repertory Group preceded the Federal Theatre. I was one of the originators of the Chicago Workers' Theatre that became the Chicago Repertory Group, 505 South State Street, third floor. We changed the name because we had just gotten the rights to do *Waiting for Lefty* from the Group Theatre in New York. They suggested that maybe it wouldn't be too wise to go with the Chicago Workers' Theatre, so we took on the name Chicago Repertory Group.

The Repertory Group was nonpaying. We were a theatre of social significance presenting plays of social significance. Some of us had to make a living, too. I had a mother and father to support, so I went on and became part of the Federal Theatre. We qualified. You just went down to the relief offices. You certified. There were five of us from the Rep Group that went over and got onto the Federal Theatre.

O SAY CAN YOU SING

The first show we did with the Federal Theatre, I can't tell you the name. It was a pippin. It lasted one performance, thank goodness, and the hierarchy of the Federal Theatre came down to observe this thing. George Kondolph, Martin Burton came down, saw it, and they felt about as repulsive toward it as we did, and so they closed it down that night. Now, what they liked about the thing was that they needed manpower for a musical they were gonna do. Nine or ten months we worked on the longest-rehearsed show [laughs] in history, *O Say Can You Sing*. Joe Whitehead was the lead. Charlie and Gracie Herbert, they were a big nightclub act. Buddy Rich was a tap dancer, and he also did a little shtick with the drums. He was a wild kid. It was years later that we found out he became a drummer.

"O say, can you sing, dance, or act? / If you can, it's a well-established fact / That Uncle Sam will take you and make you / And break you into anything." That was the theme song.

We played all kinds of parts. They were making changes, rewrites, anything that you could possibly think of. We used to become so exhausted just rehearsing and rehearsing.

They were paying us a flat salary. They were gonna have to pay it to us whether we rehearsed or whether we sat there. We'd come in, and we'd check in—Bingo! We were getting paid. That's how they could do it.

TOURING FEDERAL THEATRE

You know, ninety-six dollars a month when you were earning nothing was a hell of a lot of money. Well, I thought I was in gravy when I became the supervisor of the touring company. I was up to two hundred and twenty-five dollars a month. Do you know how important that was? Especially when there were only three theatres operating in the whole of Chicago, and we toured twenty at one time. So an actor could be a great actor, but he has to be working.

I was supervisor of the first touring company of the Federal Theatre. They had given me the headquarters in Peoria. The first show we were doing—I was one of the leads—was *Boy Meets Girl* at the Majestic Theatre. About two days before we opened, I wandered back to the box office to see how the sale of tickets were going. As I was standing there, a couple of African-Americans came up and wanted to buy two tickets. So the box office man says, "Sure," and he reaches up to the gallery. "What are you doing?" I says. "There are loads of seats here on the main floor."

He said, "Mister Peters, we can't do that." I said, "What do you mean you can't do that? I'm doing it. Here are two tickets."

So he says, "I'll have to report that." I said, "Do whatever you want to do."

I went back to my office, and about half an hour later, there was a phone call for me—Mr. Congressman Everett McKinley Dirksen: "You can't do that." I says, "The hell I can't; I just did it, and I'll do it again."

"Well, we're gonna see about that," he said. I said, "Do whatever you want to do. I'm telling you, as long as I'm here, that is what the policy is gonna be."

So they reported me to Miss Flanagan. She called me and said, "You're absolutely right. You do what you're doing. I will back you up on that."

THE "SWING" MIKADO

There I was in Peoria with my project, and Harry Minturn came down. He says, "Al, I gotta talk to you. I've got an idea. I want to run it by you. What do you think of this? Look, I've got this whole batch of black actors here, and I don't know what to do with 'em. Now, I was thinking maybe we'd take this and jazz it up a little bit. You know: We could use the swing, the swing thing." And so I says, "Hey, sounds real good."

So they decided to call it *The "Swing" Mikado*.[26] Then, of course, Mike Todd wanted to buy it, but the government couldn't sell it to him. They couldn't stop him from doing it. Mike Todd opened in New York, called it *The Hot Mikado*, but it was *The Swing Mikado* done right here at the Blackstone Theatre in Chicago, loads of seats here on the main floor.

Nobody there saw live theatre. Here is money being spent, and they are not getting theatre unless they came up to Chicago to see the Federal Theatre. So we brought theatre to them. We had advance people go out to sell the shows. We had three shows. There was *Ah Wilderness*, *Waiting for Lefty*, and *Boy Meets Girl*. So we would offer any organization—PTA group, American Legion, any one of 'em—for a fantastically little price, they could hire us. We would come in with our truck and the three union members. There were no union stipulations there.

As a matter of fact, outside of the Majestic Theatre in Peoria, we didn't play another union theatre. We would play auditoriums. You know how tough it was to do a change in a high school auditorium? It was ridiculous. We played everything. We did a tent show outdoors. For six weeks or so, we were touring our Chautauqua tent.

The audiences used to look in awe at us as we came out. They'd wait until we came out, not for autographs but to look at a live actor. They laughed when they were supposed to laugh.

Many people were on the Federal Theatre that really wouldn't have been in a professional theatre, and yet there were many people that were very, very good. Burt Lancaster, Orson Welles, E.G. Marshall—he was here in Chicago with us.

Katherine Dunham was on the Federal Theatre with us—beautiful, beautiful work. It was sensuous. Her group, the Katherine Dunham Dancers, did Caribbean dances. She was quite different from what Kurt and Grace Graff were doing and what Berta Ochsner was doing and what Ruth Paige was doing.

Sometimes we were packed. It depended on how much promotion the organization that had purchased the evening was putting behind it. If they didn't promote it, we played to half houses. I think they appreciated what they saw, not for its artistic value but for the fact that there were live people there. We were real. There was that quality. We felt that; we really did.

UNION TROUBLES

We had some of the worst Girdlers here. Do you remember the name Tom Girdler? We had a massacre here in south Chicago. Union members were out there on the line. This was Republic Steel [Girdler was company chairman]. The union members came out, and women with their babies. They had the police there. The goons lined up, and they killed eight or ten of 'em.

They crossed the line, and there was a tremendous mass meeting at the Civic Opera House. We had loads of unrest. These were the formative years of unions. CIO [Congress of Industrial Organizations] was just coming onto the floor then. The AFL [American Federation of Labor] was worthless, and even Equity didn't back us up. They were all antiunion, and so we decided this was ridiculous 'cause we were working at ten o'clock in the morning, and we'd rehearse all afternoon, then we'd have a performance that night, and we worked and worked and worked.

We said, "Hell, we ought to do something about at least getting an actors' union." Well, we weren't allowed to, but we muttered, and finally Harry Mintern says, "All right, we'll call a meeting of all the people on the show at the Blackstone Theatre. You can speak your mind and take a vote." There may have been fifteen of us at the most that were really actively trying to promote the union.

All of a sudden, we looked around, there are an awful lot of people we didn't even recognize—tough-looking guys. They were really becoming very, very aggressive. Harry Mintern got up, said, "Okay, it sounds as if there's not gonna be any unions, so this thing is all dismissed. No union."

It lasted six months, till they closed the whole thing down. First of all, they took off all the nonrelief people. All this time, they agitated. They were investigating. They were screening stuff. They hated what we were saying. *Triple-A Plowed Under* drove them crazy. *Cradle Will Rock* drove 'em crazy. The government just didn't want this all aired that way. The Dies Committee kept accusing Hallie Flanagan of the finances coming from Moscow; we used to laugh about "Moscow gold." In the Repertory Group, we didn't have a dime to our names. We had to put ten cents apiece a month to pay for the electric bill, all right? We used to laugh because the Hearst papers were talking about the Moscow gold. We'd say, "Well, where? Maybe we can steer some of this Moscow gold our way, because we haven't got a dime."

The irony of it was that there were all the boondoggling charges, but this was primarily a project for relief.

❖   ❖   ❖

Not long after this interview took place in 2001, ALAN PETERS *died in Chicago, the city he loved.*

JOHN RANDOLPH

CHILDREN'S THEATRE UNIT, NEW YORK

I've never been in anything like that. We had children hopping onstage and straightening out the actors on where they should go.

I was enthusiastic about anything. I read books about acting. I never saw a show in my life. I went in, and they said, "Won't you sit down?" I was not afraid. I had seen the story of a famous Yiddish actor, Paul Muni. He was a gangster. I didn't know what I was doing, but they gave me a sheet of paper. I just looked at it and started to talk like Paul Muni [laughs]. I talked till they gave me a job.

I got a paper from the Federal Theatre to report to a certain place. Two weeks later I got a call from the government, saying that they were accepting me for the theatre for the Arts Projects. Before I knew it, I had a job for twenty-six dollars and thirty-three something.

I worked for the first time, three times a week at night, and I could do things I loved to do. You were allowed to do what you believed in. I loved the excitement; I loved the fact that there were people to talk about acting. We met people from all over. Suddenly, scripts were coming down from writers. They were not famous. I was interested. I read everything. Beautiful actors, good actors, lousy actors—it didn't make any difference. Some were young people; some were guys like us who just got in with the business. You were told to just go ahead and do it.

One time we worked with a group of actors who were with a Suitcase Theatre.[27] You went from one part of the Bronx to the other part of the Bronx and did shows at a bar.

When we started to do shows on the air, I got one of the first jobs, and I was very proud of it. I learned how to speak twenty-some languages. I did it by research in the Bronx. If you know about the Bronx, we had little groups that came from the old country. I said, "I'm just here; I'm not a spy. I'm just here to find out where you come from and how you speak."

It wasn't that clear when we first joined the group that you were just an actor accepted by the government. Some were from Equity, and there was a big fight. Equity at first didn't want people like myself. We were just young kids. I was not really a legitimate actor. Equity made a big stink and tried to break up the group. Jules Dassin directed me, and I began to work and rehearse. Once I was in rehearsal, I decided I would like to join Equity some way, but I didn't have any credit.

As far as I knew, there was a group of people who wanted you to go and fight for people who were hungry. They also worked with the working people. I did not consider myself a working person. I was the son of a Jewish guy who gave me a phony name. I did work with the Workers' Alliance.[28]

REVOLT OF THE BEAVERS

I had never done any shows, any children's shows or anything like that. I was a beaver. I put on my own beaver face. The story is that there were bad guys—that was me [laughs]—then there were the good guys, and we kept 'em down. Julie [Jules Dassin] was a very good beaver who helped the beavers who had no food. In the meantime, there was one guy who was the owner, and he sat in a big barber chair, and he could turn around and look at all of the people and kill anybody he wanted.

I thought it was a creative thing that the king of the beavers was a son-of-a-gun who was always wretched. Guys like me had roller skates. I was only one of three villains. I've never been in anything like that. We had children hopping onstage and straightening out the actors on where they should go. You saw Julie running up and down the aisle. There was that kind of variety. The biggest price was twenty-five cents, and if you were poor, then you didn't have to give anything.

It was a wonderful play. It had songs in it. We didn't think it was a communist thing. It was just a good old drama, and we had music. We heard that there were criticisms on the show when we opened at a theatre on

Fifty-second Street. The reviews were pretty bad. I couldn't believe that Brooks Atkinson was hurt by whatever reason.

I worked with people that I never worked with after the war. Young people, old people. There was no question of whether you were black or white. They were part of the Federal Theatre.

❖   ❖   ❖

JOHN RANDOLPH, *born Emanuel Hirsch Cohen in 1915, was a blacklisted actor during the McCarthy era. He had left New York to seek a career in Hollywood. After a distinguished film career, which had resumed in the sixties, he returned to New York to win a Tony Award in 1987 for his performance in Neil Simon's* Broadway Bound. *His career of over fifty years includes Arthur Miller's* American Clock; Serpico; Conquest of the Planet of the Apes; Gaily, Gaily; All the President's Men; King Kong; *and TV's* Seinfeld *and* Touched by an Angel.

STUDS TERKEL

FEDERAL THEATRE, CHICAGO

Well, at this gathering, the audience, the striking union, they took it for real. So this guy runs down the street, and they're starting to beat up the actor. We had to holler out, "It's a play! It's a play! He's an actor! He's an actor!"

CHICAGO, THE 1920S

My mother ran a men's hotel. Back in those days, in the late twenties before the crash, a men's hotel was not a flophouse. These were old retired guys and railroad firemen, and men of vinegar works, and guys who were carpenters. That hotel was close to the Loop, the theatrical section. As a result, the old-time press agents—"advance men," they were called—would go to all the hotels and put in signs. They came to our hotel, put up a sign of a play, and I'd get two free tickets. I became a theatregoer at the age of thirteen.

I saw how the Depression affected the lives of all of us—before the Crash, no vacancies. Guys worked five-and-a-half days a week, paid on Saturday. They'd be there in the lobby Saturday night and get a few drinks. Sunday they'd visit the girls in the cribs nearby. That was pretty much it.

Then came the Depression. The next thing you know, guys are in the hotel all day. Now they no longer have jobs, and they start fighting each other. The Wall Street Crash was the official beginning of the Depression. There was an agricultural depression before that, but with the official Crash, plants closed, jobs were lost, and so these guys at the hotel were now there all day instead of just evenings, Saturday afternoons, and Sundays. When you're all day idle and you feel no good, not worthy, you start getting into scraps. They got drunk and got in fights, so that's the role the Depression played in the lives of many people.

Of course the moral is, once you're not working, you're on relief, which was welfare then. You didn't use those phony phrases like "the pathology of the subclass" or stuff like that, 'cause too many people were overwhelmingly white.

We didn't lose the hotel. It still survived, but by that time we moved on. From then on the nature of the Depression's effect on people had an effect on me and the way I thought and what I did.

I went to the University of Chicago Law School. We'll forget that, the three bleakest years of my life. I dreamed of Clarence Darrow, and I woke up to Julius Hoffman. He was [later] the judge of the Conspiracy Eight Trial.[29] "Mr. Magoo," Abbie Hoffman called him.

THE CHICAGO REPERTORY GROUP

I met this guy who was a director of plays. By this time, remember, I was a the-atre aficionado 'cause I went to plays near the hotel. This guy is the director of a play called *Waiting for Lefty* by Clifford Odets, being done by a labor group called the Chicago Repertory Group.[30] I'd never dreamed of being an actor. My dream was to be a spectator, to see plays, to see ball games, and to read a book or two and see movies.

Instead, he says, "Get up onstage—a guy didn't show up." I read a role, and he says, "You got the part." Never acted—the first thing I was ever in onstage ever was *Waiting for Lefty*. This group was a left-wing–inclined sort of group but had a huge following with theatre of "social significance." It had a large following of trade unions all over the city but also literate people and intellectuals.

Then this director says, "You know, there's a lot of soap operas in Chicago, radio soap operas. Why don't you audition for them?" I remem-bered I saw Joe Downing in *Dead End* as Baby Face Martin, and so I audi-tioned using these voices. I became a gangster in radio soap operas, the dumb gangster.

Women in White was about a nurse, *Guiding Light* was about a minister—same script—and Mary Norton suffered Mondays through Fridays, courtesy of Oxydol, more than St. Sebastian ever did. *Helen Trent:* "Can a woman find love after thirty-five?"—tells you how long ago that was. That's how I became an actor.

Movies like Busby Berkeley's films and *Broadway Follies of* so-and-so were still a diversion that was needed. Herman Shumlin directed *Grand Hotel*, Vicki Baum's novel, and it was a smash during the depths of the Depression. I specifically remember his telling me that Depression or no Depression, they packed them in that theatre. People needed something. There's always that diversion or that something light and gay or even, even enthralling. *Dinner at Eight* was a big one. That was about wealthy people.

A THEATRE OF *SOCIAL* SIGNIFICANCE

Here's where the Federal Theatre came in. Plays were not about wealthy people; they were about issues. *The Cradle Will Rock* was about a steel strike, an opera by Marc Blitzstein. The thing that was interesting about Federal Theatre were the experiments, as well. The Living Newspaper—we call it multimedia today—were the use of newsreels, of still photographs, live actors, music, song, and there were issues brought forth about the New Deal. One was called *Triple-A Plowed Under.* Another was called *Spirochete,*[31] about the attack on syphilis, written by Arnold Sundberg. *Power* was another.

The [Federal] Theatre probably was the most controversial of all by the nature of the plays they were doing. Our group, the Repertory Group, had some Federal Theatre members. We did *The Cradle Will Rock, One-Third of a Nation*—based upon the Roosevelt second inaugural address: "I see one third of a nation ill fed, ill clothed, ill housed"—but ours was different than New York's. Ours was about the Chicago Fire and the wooden houses and what happened after that. A couple of members of our group wrote the script based upon the New York script. I was the little guy, the man on the street going through it.

Of course, we know that Katherine Dunham of the dance project introduced Caribbean music to the United States, especially Haitian music. We know that Orson Welles at the age of twenty-two, twenty-three directed a black *Macbeth* with Jack Carter that had all sorts of implications to it. Welles of course is one of those protean figures that comes along once in every ten generations. To think of people who came out of it, names now forgotten, it was more than a proving ground for actors.

The stuff was rich. There were several African-American plays: *Big White Fog* by Ted Ward, a Chicago playwright. There was *Awake and Sing*, done by a Yiddish theatre group in Chicago. That was the play by Clifford Odets that the Group Theatre did. It was their first big, serious hit aside from *Waiting for Lefty*. We had *The Swing Mikado*, in which Mahalia Jackson tried out for the chorus, but her voice was too strong.

It was exciting. There was a tingle to it. There was a phrase, a Billy Rose phrase: "Want to hear me put bubbles in your blood?" The Federal Shakespeare Theatre had Ian Keith, a wonderful Shakespearean actor but a bottle baby, an alcoholic. Keith would have too much to drink and then forget lines. The stage manager would give him one line, and "Wang!"—he'd go back to the play like a house on fire. So, it had that sort of excitement to it. And it was only two bits.

Federal Theatre was played before people who had never seen plays before, had never seen live actors before. I think Hallie Flanagan recalled a Federal Theatre group doing *Twelfth Night* somewhere in a small town in the South. They're finishing, and the audience is dead silent, so they think they flopped. Then bit by bit, townspeople come to their dressing rooms bashfully, and they say, "We loved it." "Well, what happened? We didn't hear your applaud?"

"We didn't want to interrupt you." They had never seen live actors. So live theatre came to these people in small communities.

Gilbert Moses tells of doing *Waiting for Godot*. They were told it's going to be a light comedy because Burt Lahr was in it. Black sharecroppers of little education were [watching]. They recognized Lucky the slave; they recognized guys waiting, waiting, waiting. They recognized all this, and so they saw themselves. Federal Theatre reflected, in its own way and in its own time, something rich and vibrant happening.

The Chicago Repertory Group did something called Mobile Theatre. That was the phrase used for the street theatre of today. We would go out on picket lines or in soup kitchens. Some of our guys wrote scripts. The famous newspaper strike that established the Newspaper Guild in Chicago, against the Hearst paper, *The Herald Examiner*, went on a hundred and some days. During that strike we'd do sketches in the soup kitchen where the striking newspaper guys were.

THE MEMORIAL DAY MASSACRE

In 1937 in Chicago, a day known as the Memorial Day Massacre, the CIO was being organized. John L. Lewis's mine workers put up some of the money, and they organized mine workers, autoworkers, railroad workers, farm equipment workers. The steel workers' union was then called Steel Workers Organizing Committee. Big Steel finally accepted the union—that is, Carnegie, U.S. Steel, Bethlehem—but some of Republic Steel said, "No, we'll never recognize the union." A man named Tom Girdler was the head of it.

Chicago had a big Republic Steel plant on the South Side of Chicago. Memorial Day in 1937, the strikers said they were going to hold a picnic on those grounds, and they did. There was fried chicken, potato salad, women, kids, songs, baseball, and there were some cops there. Girdler had called Chicago cops, waiting for some riot to happen. Nothing was happening. Someone threw a stone, and cops started shooting—shot ten guys in the back, and they killed those ten guys. That became known as the Republic Steel Massacre.

The town was furious, and the next day about four of us went down to Sam's Place, which is a tavern, and it was like a scene out of Matthew Brady's Civil War. There they were—wounded, different guys with bandages—and we did a sketch. We did a scene from *Waiting for Lefty* and a couple of songs, and a guy read a poem. Other players were doing some dance in union halls.

Once we did *Waiting for Lefty* before a group of striking taxicab drivers. Actually, the play's about a taxicab drivers' strike. It was so thrilling, except for one problem. There's a guy in the play who's a fink, and he says, "This guy is the company union guy, and he's my own lousy brother." The guy runs down the aisle, disappears. Well, at this gathering, the audience, the striking union, they took it for real. So this guy runs down the street, and they're starting to beat up the actor. We had to holler out, "It's a play! It's a play! He's an actor! He's an actor!" He was real.

Would there have been a revolution? Well, one thing is certain: The New Deal helped people get jobs, gave them self-esteem. Ronnie Reagan's father got a job on the WPA; he was saved by the WPA. That's what I mean by "grandchildren and the children of those who condemn it most": Their granddaddies' butts were saved by the New Deal, by governmental intervention. As to whether there'd be a revolution or not, it's up for grabs. There would have been trouble, certainly.

Who was the right wing? Is it a person? Is it a thing? Is it General Motors? Is it Henry Ford? Or is it the Ford Company? You start thinking power. Remember, they had it going pretty good without unions. Unions come in, and all of a sudden there's less power than they had. Ford paid five bucks a day, which was a big one. He'd hire a bunch of spies, ex-thugs, to spy on these guys and their lives. To them a union means, "This is mine. This is my divine right, this thing that I have and own. Who are you guys? You just produce this stuff."

A union comes and says, "We gotta be together and get organized." That, in a sense, is what [the thirties Right] worried about, not revolution—just the fact they were losing power over things.

There was a feeling of excitement that the Federal Theatre represented that there was something exhilarating in the midst of all the adversity. There was a juice. I suppose the word is "a time of great juiciness."

I was interviewing a wise man of Wall Street [Bernard Baruch] to explain the Wall Street Crash to me. He was the senior partner of Goldman Sachs, leading investment banker, advisor to presidents—to Truman, to LBJ, and to JFK. I said, "What happened?" He said, "I don't know." He says, "The ticker tape was going on all night, and J.P. Morgan and John D. Junior are buying thousands. Then guys were jumping out of windows. We waited for some kind of announcement."

And I thought to myself, From whom? From God? Well, the announcement came from the big, big government. So, the very ones who condemn big government today, their daddies' and granddaddies' asses were saved by big government. And that's the part that disturbs me. We suffer more like what I call a National Alzheimer's Disease. There's no yesterday; it's forgotten.

And Federal Theatre—remembering that, remembers all the excitement and possibilities that were there.

FEAR OF COMMUNISM AND
IT CAN'T HAPPEN HERE

This fear of communism was a phony one. Of course, many people did join the Communist Party. They joined because they felt, "Geez, something has to be done, because this is not working and Russia seems great!" It turned out of course to be a nightmare. Many of those people who sympathized were those that were active in these movements of the street, Workers' Alliance, or the troops that were organizing the unions. They're for very American purposes: the right to organize, the right to a life of some dignity and some security.

Sinclair Lewis wrote a play called *It Can't Happen Here*. What if fascism came to America? It can't happen here. There's a "Silvershirt" movement going on. I was in that play in Washington, at the Washington Civic Theatre. Dave Tuttle was the director. I did Shad Ledue. He was sort of the George Wallace figure, a handyman, very bitter. The hero of the play is named Doremus Jessup, his boss, a rather aristocratic publisher who's enlightened. I hate his guts.

Now I remember the feeling from playing it. I'm a corporal. I have the uniform on suddenly, instead of my overalls, and my God—what a feeling, looking out in charge. I was empowered. I looked to the last row way back in the Wardman Park Hotel, and it was a little Mussolini-like. I remember even my chin going up that way. I'm a short guy, and I was empowered. It was mar-velous, that feeling I had, what a uniform can do. It gives you a feeling of power and getting those bastards who you think are responsible, who look down upon you as nothing.

Sometimes there's that feeling of these barbarians who do things instead of recognizing, Hey, there's something hurting here; something hurts. Shad represented all that. And that's what Sinclair Lewis had in mind.

When it came under attack by the Dies Committee, which was an early form of the House Un-American Activities Committee, Hallie Flanagan of course was called before it. Everett Dirksen was senator from Illinois. He had this plum-rich voice; I can't imitate it, one of those nice, good-natured, won-derful voices. [Imitates him:] "Well, I believe in theatre, of course. I love the-atre. I remember seeing Maude Adams in a play. I like theatre but not Federal Theatre."

THE LEGACY

Why don't we have a national theatre? Of course we should have a national theatre. We don't because we're still primitive in that respect. We're still haunted by the phrase *Government*. We're America. We're a land of individ-uals. We still think, By God, I can get that brass ring, and if I don't, it's my fault. Of course we need a national theatre. We need governmental aid whenever there's need for it.

I think Federal Theatre was a rescuer. What would have happened to theatre itself? There would have been a shambles. During those moments when people have no dough and couldn't afford theatre prices, they could come in for twenty-five cents and see something real and alive. The real playgoers aren't the wealthy sitting down there. They're the kind of people who were librarians and teachers who sit up in the galleries.

That story of sharecroppers in the South, all those rural people seeing *Twelfth Night* and being moved by it, tells you that there is awareness, there's a hunger. There's a hunger for beauty. Basically, what it amounts to is hunger for beauty. And that's what the Federal Theatre satisfied in its way.

The legacy to me is very simple. The Federal Theatre proved that there is a hunger for good, alive, pertinent theatre in this country, no matter where it's performed. There's room for it, and it's exciting. When you leave a play, it's not something you forget.

❖   ❖   ❖

Pulitzer Prize-winning author **STUDS TERKEL** *is the inspiration for* Voices from the Federal Theatre. *His collected oral histories, from* Hard Times *to* The Good War *to* Working, *preserve the voices of generations and their places in history. His most recent work,* May the Circle Be Unbroken, *is his tenth book. In the words of John Kenneth Galbraith, "Studs Terkel, as we all know, is our window on the world we don't know."*

PART I NOTES

[1]**Elia Kazan** (b. 1909) is a director, actor, and one of the original Group Theatre members. His work for stage includes *A Streetcar Named Desire* (1947), *Death of a Salesman* (1949), *Cat on a Hot Tin Roof* (1955), and *Sweet Bird of Youth* (1959). He won Academy Awards for directing *Gentleman's Agreement* (1948) and *On the Waterfront* (1954); he was also nominated for *East of Eden* (1955) and the film version of *A Streetcar Named Desire* (1951). His decision to name fellow artists in 1952 during the HUAC hearings has caused controversy over the years.

[2]**Heywood Broun** (1888–1939) was a sports reporter, a war correspondent, and a columnist. In his *New York World* column "It Seems to Me," he championed the underdog, criticizing social injustice, racial discrimination, and censorship. In 1933 he helped establish the Newspaper Guild, which played a paramount role in the creation of the Federal Theatre's Living Newspapers.

[3]***Stevedore*** (1936) was typical of the plays chosen by the Negro Unit in Washington state. Theodore Brown, a member of the Negro Unit in Seattle, described *Stevedore*, written by George Sklar and Paul Peters, as "a play whose universal theme remains the same regardless of race or creed."

[4]**The Group Theatre** was founded in 1931 by Harold Clurman, Lee Strasberg, and Cheryl Crawford. It was a collective of theatre artists who based their work on the "sense-memory" techniques of Stanislavksy's Moscow Art Theatre and dedicated themselves to presenting new American plays of

social significance. The Federal Theatre presented such Group Theatre plays as Clifford Odets's *Waiting for Lefty* and *Awake and Sing* (1935).

[5]*Revolt of the Beavers* (1937). New York critic Brooks Atkinson called the play "*Mother Goose Marx*," while Hallie Flanagan defended it as only a fairy tale. It would later be used as evidence in the HUAC hunt for communists in the Federal Theatre.

[6]**A Marriage Proposal** (1936) was based on the play by Anton Chekhov.

[7]*Life and Death of an American* (1939), written by John Sklar, was called "the most superb stage production in America." It centered around Jerry Dorgan, "first kid of the 20th century, born at twelve seconds past midnight, born to grow with America, with the century." In the words of its main character, "Everybody counts."

[8]**Jean Rosenthal** (1912–1969) began her career as an assistant to Abe Feder with Orson Welles and John Houseman on the Federal Theatre Project. She went on to become the lighting and production supervisor for Martha Graham. Her Broadway designs included *West Side Story* and *The Sound of Music*.

[9]**The Artef** emerged in the 1920s and 1930s. It was a proletarian theatre organization affiliated with the American Communist movement. Its radical politics shaped the productions, which continued until its demise in 1940.

[10]*The Emperor's New Clothes* (1938) was written by Charlotte Chorpenning and directed in New York by Maurice Clark. Sam Bonnell, a seasoned Broadway actor, played Zan to Jules Dassin's Zar. During its one-and-a-half-year run, it played to over a quarter of a million people.

[11]**Medicine Show** was produced by Martin Gabel, who married Arlene Francis, a member of the Federal Theatre Project. She later joined Orson Welles's Mercury Theatre.

[12]**Bill "Bojangles" Robinson** achieved fame as a nightclub and musical comedy performer, becoming the toast of Broadway. Toward the end of the

vaudeville era, he appeared in *Blackbirds of 1928*, a black revue for white audiences. After 1930, Robinson appeared in fourteen motion pictures, most frequently opposite Shirley Temple in the stereotypical role of a butler. In 1939 he returned to the Broadway stage in *The Hot Mikado*, a jazz version of the Gilbert and Sullivan operetta produced at the 1939 New York World's Fair and based on the Federal Theatre production of *The "Swing" Mikado*.

[13]**Canada Lee** (born Leonard Canegata, 1907–1952) was one of the foremost African-American actors to come out of the Federal Theatre. He played Blacksnake in the 1934 production of *Stevedore*, Banquo in the Federal Theatre's *"Voodoo" Macbeth* (1936), and Emperor Christophe in *Haiti* (1938). Lee went on to a successful career, portraying Bigger Lee in Richard Wright's *Native Son* in 1941, among many other roles.

[14]**Joseph Losey** (1909–1964). After graduating from Harvard, Losey went to study with Bertolt Brecht in Germany. Returning to New York, he made his debut in 1936, directing the first of the agitprop Living Newspapers. After the war his Hollywood film-directing career was destroyed when he was named as a Communist by HUAC. Blacklisted, Losey moved to England, where he continued his impressive film career, collaborating with Pinter on such films as *The Servant* and *The Go-Between*.

[15]*Triple-A Plowed Under* (1936), a Living Newspaper, was an exposé of the poor, substandard living conditions of America's urban populations.

[16]**Arthur Arent** (1904–1972) created the FTP's Living Newspapers with the head of the New York Newspaper Guild, Morris Watson, and a team of writers and researchers.

[17]**Virgil Thomson** (1896–1989) studied in Paris with Nadia Boulanger, where he also met Cocteau, Stravinsky, Satie, and the artists of Les Six. He composed in almost every genre, from opera to jazz to film.

[18]*Injunction Granted* (1936) was a Living Newspaper on the history of labor in the courts.

[19]**Morris Watson** supervised the Living Newspaper Unit, sponsored by the New York Newspaper Guild. Set up like a city daily, the unit was run by an editor-in-chief, managing editor, and city editor, who worked with reporters and copyreaders to dramatize the news.

[20]*Power* (1937), a Living Newspaper, dramatized the need for affordable electric power for the ordinary consumer.

[21]*One-Third of a Nation* (1938), a Living Newspaper that was performed by ten of the Federal Theatre units across the country, was adapted to the urban living conditions in each city. Written by Arthur Arent and the Living Newspaper staff, the play depicted life in New York City slums. The title was taken from a line in Roosevelt's second inaugural address: "I see one-third of a nation ill-housed, ill-clad, and ill-nourished."

[22]**Howard Bay** (1912–1986) was a stage and film designer whose career was launched with the realistic, seventy-foot-tall tenement set for the Federal Theatre Project's *One-Third of a Nation.* He went on to design *The Little Foxes, Show Boat, The Music Man, Finian's Rainbow,* and *Man of La Mancha* on Broadway.

[23]*Horse Eats Hat* (1936), based on a French farce, *Un chapeau de paille d'Italie* by Eugene Labiche, was produced by Houseman's and Welles's Project 891. It was translated, directed, and acted in by Orson Welles. Nat Karson designed the scenery and costumes, and Virgil Thomson composed the score.

[24]*Sing for Your Supper* (1939) was one of the final productions playing when the Federal Theatre died. It was created by the Project Staff and included the stirring "Ballad for Americans," originally titled "Ballad for Uncle Sam."

[25]**"Ballad for Americans,"** originally sung in *Sing for Your Supper,* was later performed by Paul Robeson and the New York Philharmonic and chosen as the theme song of the Republican National Convention in Philadelphia in 1940. It was sung at the Adelphi Theatre on the last night of the Federal Theatre by the project that originated it.

[26]**The "Swing" Mikado** (1938). By January 1939 *The Swing Mikado* had become the hit of the season in Chicago. Everyone wanted to buy the production; however, WPA executives would not sell. Among the commercial offers was that of Mike Todd, who would later produce the show on Broadway as *The Hot Mikado*, starring Bill "Bojangles" Robinson.

[27]**Suitcase Theatre** traveled from community to community. It was not confined to the countryside. In Brooklyn, the Bronx, and Manhattan, the truck would roll up, the sides would drop down, and the truck would become a mini-stage where people would gather to watch the play.

[28]**Workers' Alliance**, created in 1934, was a union of WPA and PWA workers that sought to organize the Federal Arts Projects.

[29]At the **Conspiracy Eight**, or Chicago Eight, Trial (1969–72), eight radicals—among them Abbie Hoffman, Jerry Rubin, and Tom Hayden—were accused of conspiring to incite a riot at the 1968 Democratic Convention in Chicago to highlight their opposition to the Vietnam War.

[30]**Waiting for Lefty** (1935) was developed by Clifford Odets and the Group Theatre and adopted by Federal Theatre units across the country. First performed as a Sunday benefit for the League of Workers' Theatres' *New Theatre* magazine, it became the signature 1930's agitprop theatre piece.

[31]**Spirochete** (1938) was a Living Newspaper focusing on the history of syphilis. Endorsed by the surgeon general of the United States Public Health Service, it was performed throughout the country.

Perry Bruskin, New York, 2000

Federal Theatre for Children, Central Park, New York, circa 1937

Revolt of the Beavers, Adelphi Theatre, New York, 1937

LIFE AND DEATH OF AN AMERICAN

a new play
by
GEORGE SKLAR

Evenings (exc. Mon.) at 8:40   Saturday matinee at 2:40

Evenings 25¢ to $1.10   Matinees 25¢ to 83¢

For theatre parties at special rates, call GRamercy 7-7800, ext. 56

MAXINE ELLIOTT'S THEATRE
39th Street, East of Broadway

Printed by Publications Division, National Service Bureau

Life and Death of an American, New York, 1939

Arthur Kennedy in *Life and Death of an American*, 1939

Jules Dassin, New York, 2000

Jules Dassin, 1936

Jules Dassin (right) as Zan in *The Emperor's New Clothes*,
New York, 1936

Jules Dassin (center) in *Revolt of the Beavers*, Adelphi
Theatre, New York, 1937

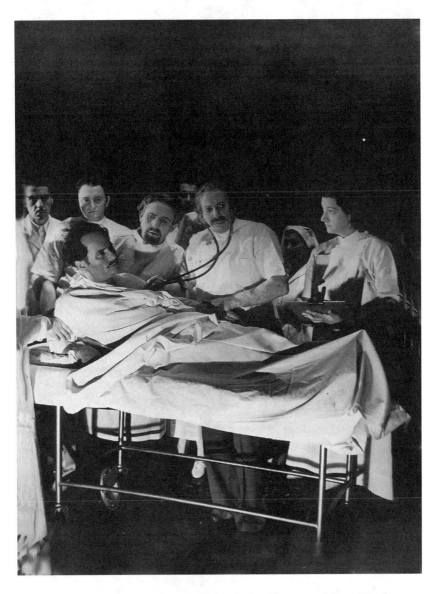

Medicine Show, directed by Jules Dassin, New York

Congressman Martin Dies, chairman of HUAC, 1939

Martin Dies and the Dies Committee, Washington, D.C., 1939

Professor Mamlock, Yiddish Theatre Unit, Massachusetts, 1938

Rosetta LeNoire, Connecticut, 2001

Rosetta in the *"Voodoo" Macbeth,* Negro Theatre Unit,
Harlem, 1936

Opening night at the Lafayette Theatre, 1936

Canada Lee, circa 1936

Norman Lloyd, Los Angeles, 2000

Norman Lloyd in *Injunction Granted*, Biltmore Theatre,
New York, 1936

Triple-A Plowed Under, New York, 1936

Orson Welles in *The Tragical History of Dr. Faustus*,
Lafayette Theatre, New York, 1937

One-Third of a Nation, New York, 1938

Horse Eats Hat, Project 891, New York, 1936

Sing for Your Supper, New York, 1939

Power, New York, 1939

Alan Peters, Chicago, 2000

Alan Peters (right), director of FTP Touring Unit, Chicago, circa 1936

Alan Peters studying *Black Pit* script, Chicago, 1936

Chicago Repertory Theatre with Alan Peters, 1930s

The *"Swing" Mikado*, Great Northern Theatre,
Chicago, 1938

Boy Meets Girl, Majestic Theatre, Peoria, 1937

John Randolph, Los Angeles, 2000

Revolt of the Beavers with John Randolph, Biltmore Theatre, New York, 1937

Set design for *Revolt of the Beavers*, New York, 1937

Studs Terkel, Chicago, 2001

It Can't Happen Here, October 27, 1936: Adelphi Theatre,
New York

It Can't Happen Here, October 27, 1936: Bridgeport,
Connecticut

It Can't Happen Here, October 27, 1936: Negro Unit,
Tacoma, Washington

It Can't Happen Here, October 27, 1936: Yiddish Unit,
Biltmore Theatre, New York, with Sidney Lumet as the boy

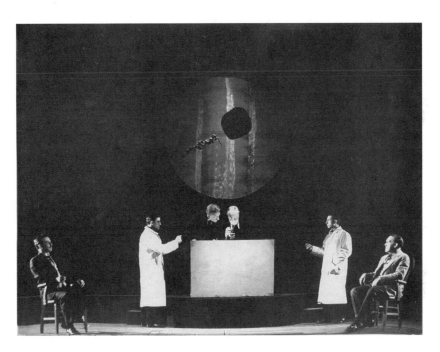

Spirochete, Chicago, 1938

THE
PRODUCERS

JOHN HOUSEMAN

NEGRO THEATRE UNIT

PROJECT 891, NEW YORK

Naturally, if you get a few actors, a few theatre people, together and give them a roof over their heads and enough to eat, they're liable to create miracles, which is exactly what happened.

E verybody was starving to death. As you know, there were eighteen million unemployed, and the arts projects were a very tiny fraction of the whole WPA project. The idea was wonderful. Instead of just giving people a dole, a check once a week for sitting around, Harry Hopkins, particularly, tried to create work for them in their chosen profession. It was fairly generally agreed that since we had to keep, at one time, sixteen million people alive, they might as well be doing their chosen work.

Of course, that was particularly true in the arts projects. There's no question that many of the most successful and famous of our American painters were kept alive by the Federal Arts Project. So that's how the arts projects were born, specifically the Federal Theatre, which finally, I think, was employing around fifteen or twenty thousand people all over the country.

It was simply a way of keeping people alive with a certain amount of self-respect. Naturally, if you get a few actors, a few theatre people, together and give them a roof over their heads and enough to eat, they're liable to create miracles, which is exactly what happened.

The New York theatre was in trouble. It was terribly diminished from what it had been ten years before, but that was the Depression. It never really picked up again, as it had been before talking pictures came, in the middle twenties on. The professional theatre, or the commercial theatre, was beginning to have a hard time. They were not hurt in any way by the Federal Theatre. In fact, they were helped, probably. The people who'd never been near a theatre before were now going to see shows, and that brought them into the commercial theatre, too.

In the beginning, particularly, most professional theatre people didn't see that, because some of the most bitter opposition to the Federal Theatre came from the Communist Party. In the beginning their first attitude was, this is just a way of knocking down wages; this is a nefarious project. They changed their minds, and about a year later they became great advocates of the Federal Theatre. Of course, they organized. They had really controlled the two unions that were in charge of the workers. In some ways they were sort of a nemesis.

The audiences, especially outside of New York, found themselves being offered entertainment at a very modest fee, twenty-five cents or fifty cents. These were people who'd never been to a theatre in their lives, so a whole new audience was created through the WPA, quite apart from all the other good that they did.

At about the same time as the Federal Theatre, there'd been a very distinct shift in the nature of New York audiences. The old carriage trade—the middle-class, upper-class audience that used to go to the theatre as a regular thing—was first disrupted when talking pictures came in. Then, of course, radio and the Depression had a drastic effect on all that. All these things combined. By '33, '34, the theatre had already, on its own, changed its audience to some extent. They still had the carriage trade, but they also had the new audience, which was much more left wing and much more concerned with the contemporary. Odets[1] was probably the leading playwright of that generation. Saroyan[2] was part of it, too, and there was a new audience forming.

When the Federal Theatre opened its doors, that same new audience became our audience, and a lot of new people suddenly found they could get very good entertainment for a quarter or fifty cents. That was an enormous contribution to the theatre.

HALLIE'S VISION

The really remarkable thing is the choice of Hallie[3] to head the Theatre Project. The head of the Writers' Project was perfectly predictable. So was the head of the painters and sculptors; that was perfectly predictable. These were distinguished men in their own field, but Hallie, although she achieved considerable reputation with the Vassar Experimental Theatre, was in fact totally unknown in the professional theatre. The whole thing was a thunderclap. How the hell did he [Harry Hopkins] get the notion of putting in this amateur woman? It was bad enough that she was a woman, but also she was not a theatre professional in the sense that Broadway understood it. Of course, it was the salvation of the project. She ran it brilliantly and with just that amount of nonprofessional imagination that made it work.

To Hallie the theatre all over the country was just as important as New York. When she finally got It Can't Happen Here, the Sinclair Lewis play, she opened it simultaneously in about twenty-some different theatres all over the country. The intention was to make it a national enterprise. We who worked in New York were a little inclined to think that we were the central things. Certainly, the most active and the most distinguished productions came out of New York, but not all. There were others, and on the coast they still talk about the productions that were done under the Federal Theatre.

THE NEGRO THEATRE UNIT

The "Voodoo" Macbeth came about this way. I went because of my great friendship with a very famous black actress called Rose McLendon[4] and the fact that I'd done a lot of work with blacks. I was appointed codirector with Rose. Unfortunately, she had suddenly become aware that she had very advanced cancer, and she really had very little opportunity to do anything with the theatre. However, we were so far advanced by that time that I remained in sole charge of the Negro unit, which was eight hundred people, the biggest employer of blacks in New York City. How the hell do you manage a company

of eight hundred, especially since about half of them were very dubiously connected with the theatre, anyway?

From previous experience—especially during the Virgil Thomson–Gertrude
Stein opera [*Four Saints in Three Acts*], which we did entirely with black
people—I decided the only way to deal with this was to cut the theatre into two
parts, which were not hermetically sealed; people could move if they wanted to.
One-half of the theatre was devoted to indigenous shows. We did shows written
by black authors, directed by black directors, entirely played by blacks, and
preferably on contemporary black subjects. In the other half, I decided we would
do classics, regardless of color, regardless of anything; we'd simply do the classics.
If you say you're going to do the classics, what you're really saying is you're going
to do Shakespeare.

Then the problem was to find a director, because there were no black
directors who'd had the experience or the chance ever to work in the classics.
I didn't want an Englishman. I didn't want them all talking in Oxford
accents. So I bethought me of this brilliant young man with whom I was sort
of already in partnership at the time [Orson Welles],[5] but we'd never had
enough money to produce anything. I invited him to come up to Harlem as
an experiment to see how I could work with him. He thought up the idea of
doing *Macbeth* and laying it in the Caribbean. It was an enormous success.
They loved him, and they rehearsed for a long time. It turned out to be probably one of the most successful shows that were done in the theatre that year.

There's a famous story about the critic of the *Herald Tribune*, Percy
Hammond. When we did the *Voodoo Macbeth*, it was very successful, and we
got very nice reviews except from a few die-hard Republican papers. Percy
Hammond wrote a perfectly awful review saying this was a disgrace that
money was being spent on these people who couldn't even speak English and
didn't know how to do anything. It was a dreadful review but purely a political review.

We had in the cast of *Macbeth* about twelve voodoo drummers and one
magic man, a medicine man who used to have convulsions on the stage every
night. They decided that this was a very evil act by Mr. Hammond, and they
came to Orson and me and showed the review. They said, "This is bad man."
And we said, "Yeah, a helluva bad man. Sure, he's a bad man."

The next day when Orson and I came to the theatre, the theatre manager
said, "I don't know how to tell you this, but there were some very strange

goings-on last night. After the show they stayed in the theatre, and there was drumming and chanting and stuff." We said, "Oh, really?" What made it interesting was the fact that we'd just read the afternoon papers. Percy Hammond had just been taken to the hospital with an acute attack of something from which he died a few days later. We always were convinced that we had unwittingly killed him.

We turned that project over to the people in Harlem, and then Orson and I created a classical theatre on Broadway, which was called Project 891.

PROJECT 891

We had a very successful show, which was, strangely enough, Christopher Marlowe's *Tragedy of Doctor Faustus*.[6] To everybody's amazement, it ran for about four-and-a-half months on Broadway. Suddenly one night, unannounced, Harry Hopkins appeared in the audience, and of course, word spread immediately that he was here. At the end of the show, I invited him to come backstage and meet with Orson and I.

We were entirely concentrated on the New York Project. We never traveled. We did send out the *Voodoo Macbeth* all over the country, but that was a year-and-a-half later, and we never encountered any opposition. Remarkable as it may seem, we played the Dallas–Fort Worth State Fair. To be taking a black show into Dallas was a very audacious thing, but we had no problems. There was no censorship at all.

We continued doing very radical productions right through, and we were allowed to do it. Hallie Flanagan heard *The Cradle Will Rock* and authorized its production. She had no way of knowing that by the time we were ready to produce it, there'd be enormous industrial conflicts all over the country. There were reasons why the WPA was embarrassed at producing that play, which we ignored and pretended that we didn't understand, but we did understand perfectly.

Less than eight months later, we got into a terrible row with the WPA Federal authorities over *The Cradle Will Rock*. By that time all the arts projects, particularly the WPA, were doomed, because people kept forgetting that it was a relief measure and it was not state subsidy of a theatre.

When the WPA was liquidated, we all were very depressed, particularly in connection with the Negro situation. We felt that much of what we'd

accomplished in the way of antidiscrimination—especially among technicians and theatre workers, who had been completely banned by the theatrical union—at the end of the WPA, we had a feeling that everything was
regressing, going back to the old situation, which indeed it was, up to a point.
But the seeds had been sown, and undoubtedly the big change that took place
in the fifties[7] would not have happened had the WPA Federal Theatre not
existed.

I was very realistic about the whole thing. I knew that it was a temporary
business, that it was a relief measure. Certainly, Orson and I and a lot of our
friends used it as such. Make no bones about it: We were delighted to be serving the community, but we were also serving ourselves. Where else do you get
an opportunity to spend money to produce these wonderful shows? And we
were very proud of having done this under the aegis of the Federal Theatre.
There's no question that our careers were materially advanced by this opportunity that we were given.

❖   ❖   ❖

JOHN HOUSEMAN *(1902–1988) was born in Bucharest and*
educated in England. He began his producing career in New York in 1934.
After leaving the Federal Theatre Project, he cofounded the Mercury
Theatre with Orson Welles in 1937. He later served as artistic director for
the American Shakespeare Festival and the Drama Division of the Juilliard
School of the Performing Arts, and founded the Acting Company in New
York. He won popular acclaim playing law professor Kingsfield in the
movie The Paper Chase, *which later became a television series. He pub-*
lished four accounts of his life in the theatre, Run-Through, Front and
Center, Final Dress, *and* Unfinished Business. *This interview was done*
shortly before he died.

WOODIE KING, JR.

NEW FEDERAL THEATRE, NEW YORK

There was this unbelievable kind of resurgence of artistic energy in America from our black artists, and especially from black actors, writers, and directors.

I started the New Federal Theatre based on having studied a lot about the old Federal Theatre, and I knew a lot of the people who had worked in it.

Between 1935 and 1939, there was no theatre for black actors. They had no place to work. They might work in a small theatre in the community for free—no kind of income whatsoever, you know. Then along came Roosevelt and the Works Progress Administration, and they set up this Negro Unit of the Federal Theatre. Richard Wright, Ralph Ellison, Gwendolyn Brooks, Margaret Walker[8]—they all worked at one unit or another of the Federal Theatre Project. Suddenly, they were getting paid. It was taking people off the welfare rolls and putting them on a payroll. This gave them some sort of pride in what they were doing, gave them some sort of belief in the country, if you will.

There was this unbelievable kind of resurgence of artistic energy in America from our black artists, and especially from black actors, writers, and directors. Rose McClendon had a company called the Rose McClendon Players, and she wanted to bring her entire company in as a part of the Federal Theatre in Harlem. I think from day one those artists who were not members of it had problems.

Rose McClendon had also worked with the Group Theatre, which was heavily influenced by the radical left, Stanislavsky, and the so-called Russian implosion in America. She was indeed toying with ideas proposed by the Communist Party.

At that time I don't think there had been any black producer or director working exclusively on Broadway that had the kind of respect that the United States government would indeed sponsor or pay for. So she brought in this older, and in a sense, master, John Houseman, and he brought in the younger Orson Welles, who was sort of a prophet because the guy was a genius. At 21 or 22, he did things that I don't think any other producer-director, black or white had ever done up until that point. It also set him up to work with black artists for the next twenty, thirty years.

"THERE'S SOMETHING HAPPENING OVER AT THE LAFAYETTE ON 132ND AND SEVENTH AVENUE THAT WE WANT TO KNOW ABOUT, AND IT'S ABOUT US"

It was the first time that audiences from downtown came uptown, and audiences from uptown said, "Oh, there's something happening over at the Lafayette[9] on 132nd and Seventh Avenue that we want to know about, and it's about us." Those early photographs of people crowding outside of the theatre: They are smiling, and they are happy, and they are dressed up to go to the theatre in Harlem. So, it was a thing to do, you know. You could go to a place like the Savoy Ballroom or the Apollo or the Lincoln Theatre and see black movies, but the theatre had not grasped the imagination of the people.

According to Tommy Anderson, who was in the *Voodoo Macbeth*, he said that it was one of those experiences where everyone was so busy and in such chaos, they could not see the beauty of what he was doing. It was like pulling together fifteen or twenty people in one room and trying to get twenty ideas, but at the helm of it, Orson Welles knew what he was doing. He knew he was going to set this *Macbeth* in Haiti, around voodoo and all that. Add these drums and all of this pageantry that America saw as sort of exotic in dealing with black Americans—Orson Welles capitalized on that in putting *Macbeth* together.

The Negro Unit did *The Trial of Dr. Beck* by Hughes Allison.[10] It was a trial of a black doctor who they believed had killed his wife. His wife was like the Madame C.J. Walker[11] of that period. There were these back-and-forths about color consciousness of the period. Then came the one that we are doing now, called *Conjur Man Dies*, by Rudolf Fisher.

CONJUR MAN DIES

We are staging *Conjur Man Dies*[12] as a historical piece of work. We are staging it in honor of our theatre being the New Federal Theatre. What it will say is that in 1936 this kind of work was happening by black artists, by black writers. This is the kind of black music that they had in 1930, and people will say, "Ohhh, man, that's so beautiful."

In terms of the audiences, we want them to look at it and have the kind of fun that they had in 1936, the kind of clothes they wore at that period, the kind of hats they wore, the kind of double-breasted suits they wore, and ever so slightly, the language of the period. Now, these young people who are doing the play had no idea: "Oh, wow—you're doing a play in 1936? There was a doctor in it?" "Yeah."

"He was a graduate from Harvard?" "Yes."

"There were police detectives and all that, in addition to comics?" "Oh yeah—that's why we're doing it." [Comics were usual in black entertainment of the time; the role of detective was not.]

There were supposed to be thirty-five thousand people who saw this play in the Negro Unit in New York, New Jersey, and Chicago. [Recorded figures document eighty-three thousand in Harlem alone.] The reviewers thought it was a unique and different aspect of Negro life, you know. But these were white reviews from downtown. The *Amsterdam News* just thought it was a fun-filled, enlightening evening in the theatre.

In *Conjur Man Dies* there is a doctor, and he went to Harvard University. He got out and came back to Harlem to practice medicine. Of course, no one would go to a black doctor, so he had no way of making a living. He was out of Nigeria or Ghana, and he said, "Okay, I'll practice a certain kind of voodoo; I'll become a conjur man." He would tell people's fortune. If someone had the chicken pox, he'd say, "You have so-and-so-and-so. Take this, and you will be well," and they would get well. If they had the measles: "Oh, take this." They said, "That guy can tell fortunes; he can give us all kinds of medicine to cure us." In our mystery play the Conjur Man is killed, and two Harlem detectives set out to find out how he was killed and who killed him.

The author, Rudolph Fisher, was a medical doctor. He came from Baltimore. He graduated from Brown University and Howard University, and he wrote short stories and novels. The most interesting [story] he wrote was called "[The] City of Refuge." *Conjur Man Dies* is based on his novel [*The Conjure-Man Dies: A Mystery Tale of Dark Harlem*, 1932]. He died very young, probably before he had a chance to actually see this play done, in the mid-thirties. In that time, when he was writing, he did not write in dialect. He did not write in any kind of vernacular other than that his characters were a part of the migration from the South to the urban North.

They broke down so many stereotypes, because black people were in charge of doing these plays. *Conjur Man Dies* was actually directed by a black guy and a white guy. That had not happened in the American theatre before. Only white guys were in charge of directing or white women in charge of directing plays by blacks, okay? All these pieces were just base enough and just raw enough to transpose the jazz music of the period into an acceptable, public kind of thing.

When Orson Welles directed *Voodoo Macbeth*, his cast was almost thirty-five people; most of them were black people. Orson Welles had a sort of, like, camaraderie that most directors in America never had with that many black actors at one time.

The actors' union was just beginning in the thirties, I think. This black actor, Lee Wipper, was one of the first black actors in Actors' Equity Association. The union was very new, so it was not like they were kept out, but you had to get work in order to be a union member. If there was no work going on, you could not become a union member, and certainly the federal government, under the WPA, was not encouraging guys to come and join the union; they were just giving them work.

Big White Fog[13] was under the directorship and leadership of a very strong individual, Theodore Ward; that's why he did not last too long in the Federal Theatre Project. Ward was a part of a playwrights' unit that worked out of Henry Street here.

Plays like William Dubose's *Haiti*[14] were unbelievably large-cast plays, and they did not have the immediate visibility of an Orson Welles or John Houseman shepherding them, so they had a lot of chaos around them. The Federal Theatre was not overly concerned about that. It was not their problem. Their problem was just really having artists work and pay them to work. If you did *Haiti* for four weeks and then it closed, you go to another one. You know what I mean: "Hey, fine. Now if it all falls into chaos at the end of this run, it's gonna close. It's not gonna go anywhere." And I think that's what happened with a lot of the projects.

A lot of us think that the theatre in this country is federally funded, that the almost hundred million dollars that goes into the resident professional theatres around the United States is nothing other than a federally funded project. Now there are sophisticated ways of tracking that money and accounting for that money they did not have during the WPA.

Because the WPA took a lot of black people and put them on a payroll, for every one or two black persons they had on payroll, they had maybe fifty or sixty white people on payrolls around the country, and I think that's basically the way it is now. We get a grant for a small amount. You can bet there are fifty theatres that get almost a hundred times that from the same government, so it's not like there's a federally funded American theatre as we had in the Federal Theatre Project.

What happens in black theatre, whether it's *Conjur Man Dies* or whether it is the *Voodoo Macbeth* or *Big White Fog* or *The Trial of Doctor Beck*, is that a script comes in, and that script is either liked or not. If that script has certain problems within it, I might not be able to overcome any kind of censorship to do it. Back in the late eighties, early nineties, there was a whole brouhaha with the National Endowment about Robert Mapplethorpe and Karen Finley, but it was really about art and its relationship to the Catholic Church in America, art and its relationship to sexuality and nudity. In the black theatre, our concern is not how we will confront religion; our concern is not how we will confront our sexuality. Our concern is how we will confront the materialistic values, social, political, and economic.

I think they would just ignore us, and that is the problem with black art in America, whether it's black theatre or whatever. The system, once it acknowledges you as a human being, it must acknowledge your art. So therefore, they're not gonna acknowledge your art because they must acknowledge you.

❖   ❖   ❖

WOODIE KING, JR., *is the founder and producing director of the New Federal Theatre in New York City. Mr. King has directed on Broadway, at Ford's Theatre in Washington, D.C., and at regional theatres across the country. He has restaged* Conjur Man Dies *and* Macbeth, *two productions made popular by the original Federal Theatre of the 1930s, and has documented the FTP's Negro Theatre Unit in Harlem.*

ROBERT SCHNITZER

FEDERAL THEATRE PROJECT ADMINISTRATOR, WASHINGTON, D.C.

NORTHEAST REGIONAL DIRECTOR, TREASURE ISLAND, CALIFORNIA

The company manager said to this man, "Isn't he pretty young for Shakespeare?" And the old man said, "I want he should say he seen Shakespeare. I did once when I was a kid." Knocks me out.

DEPRESSION-ERA THEATRE

Well, I'd say the theatre was very sad in the Depression, because it was the most expensive of the entertainment arts, aside from perhaps ballet. Just about all of the performing arts suffered very severely during the Depression, and if there's no money at the box office, you can't put shows on. The movies certainly had an effect. They were a substitute for the theatre you couldn't afford. Of course, the theatre in those days was a far more popular entertainment. You could put on a show for a reasonable cost. A good, entertaining show could run half a year, make its money back and maybe a little profit.

I had the good fortune to start with Walter Hampden.[15] I'd walked on for the Theatre Guild while I was still in college. I was at Columbia, and the Theatre Guild was just a thirty-minute ride on the subway. I got my real start with Walter Hampden the year I graduated. It was a great disappointment to my father when he found that I was really going into the theatre, but I must say, I found it was useful to me all my life. I grew in Walter Hampden's Company from a walk-on to bit parts to assistant stage manager to major roles and stage manager over a period of approximately ten years. It was very fortunate for me because that was the period of the Great Depression, and he was the last of the actor-managers to have his own company. He was, even in those days before the Crash, financed, so well financed that we had a short season in New York and would then go on the road for several months.

DELAWARE FEDERAL THEATRE: "WE'RE NOT GOING TO PUT THEM BACK INTO NIGHTSHIRTS!"

I had the good fortune to have my own little summer company, a barn that we converted outside of Wilmington, Delaware. My partner and I went down there and opened a stock show. It was a resident company of about eight people who presented plays that had been hits on Broadway anywhere from last year to fifty years ago, changing weekly and doing quite a memorizing job on next week's show.

In those days, the late twenties and thirties, you didn't have to have stars. You had a basic company of eight people: two leads, two juveniles, two character people who played the grandparents, and two seconds who played everything from the villain to the uncle. If you had a larger cast, and if you were fortunate enough to start the season with a four-character play, you didn't have to bring the rest of them down until the next week. The local people followed those people. They didn't demand the stars. It was a very different picture.

I was just finishing my season at my summer theatre, and Federal Theatre had just been established. I shared a not very high opinion of what this new gadget was going to do. I was a professional, after all. I was invited by the

WPA director to come and be interviewed because they were going to establish a Federal Theatre unit in Wilmington, Delaware. Having always worked on the theory that you take the first job offered—you don't stand around waiting for somebody to give you your ideal job—I went to see him.

As the directors of WPA were usually political appointees, I expected him to ask for whom I had voted. Although I had voted for Mr. Roosevelt, I still didn't want anybody asking me how I voted, so I was surprised when he asked me just two questions, one of them did I "believe in putting people to work at their own professions, getting them back into it as soon as possible?" That was easy. I said, "Yes, of course."

And he said, "And do you think you can handle the job?" At thirty or whatever it was, to ask me that question was foolish. I said, "Of course." So I got the job as director of the Federal Theatre Unit in Wilmington, Delaware.

Each unit was formed wherever they felt there was enough theatrical unemployment to set up a theatre. Ten percent was to provide for management and spare artists and things like that, to make the thing go. The unit was responsible to Washington, probably through state director of the arts but not through the director of all WPA, which was a bone of contention, because the state directors were political appointees and didn't like not having full control. We reported, and our budgets were set in conference with the state director and finally approved by Washington. Our reports went in, copied to the state but directly to Washington every month, on what we'd been doing, what our problems were, what our successes were, how we had done it, and so on—a narrative report as well as a financial report every month.

You didn't have to ask for approval. You were trusted. You might discuss it with your state director of the arts, but you didn't put it up to Washington at all. I don't remember discussing *Caesar* with anybody. I had been told to cooperate with the board of education, and they were doing *Julius Caesar*, and so I did *Julius Caesar*.

I was given people who were not the cream, even of the unemployed actors. They were mainly old vaudevillians and old theatre actors, but none of them had brilliant careers.

I had been told to cooperate with the local education department, and they were studying *Julius Caesar*. So I thought, All right, our first show will be *Julius Caesar*. Then I looked at these people, and I thought, They can't; they'll look funny in the costume. So I thought, We'll modernize it. Mussolini was at his height, though still a friend of the United States, so I put Caesar's people into Blackshirt and Brutus's people into the khaki of democracy, and we didn't change anything in the script. We played it straight, not making fun or anything like that, but it offended a politically minded priest and his Italian congregation. He complained to Washington.

Harry Hopkins went to Hallie Flanagan and said, "Can't you put them in the costumes?" She said, "We're not going to put them back into nightshirts. If you want to, you can close it. I won't." And Hopkins didn't, and we played on.

Hallie had this very nice habit of sending out any scripts that came back to her from the field from forty different units. Any that interested her, she felt had been useful, she circulated among all the forty directors of the various units. Orson Welles got my prompt script among others and salted it away. When he went out to the Mercury Theatre—which of course was our desire, to have everybody move back into private enterprise as soon as possible—he brought it out and did it, and I confess far more brilliantly than I did.

We were successful enough for me to go back and demand that we be allowed to charge admission. You had to prove the quality of your work before you could do that. It was a sign of your maturity in the organization, of the quality of your work. You weren't allowed to charge admission till Hallie and her staff felt that you were giving a performance that was worth admission.

I was summoned to Washington. I was called down and of course wondered what was the matter. I found her, this wonderful little woman at the far end of the drawing room in an old mansion that had been taken over as the headquarters for the arts project. She had this wonderful quality of putting you at ease and bringing out the best in you. We talked about what I'd been doing, and at the end of the conversation, she said, "Well, is there something we can do for you?" And I said, "Yes, let us charge admission."

She consulted her financial advisor, who was there beside her. He said, "If you can afford it," and she said, "What else?" From then on the relationship was very satisfactory. In a while, when she lost one of her assistants, she brought me down to Washington, where I was for a year.

1939-1940 SAN FRANCISCO WORLD'S FAIR

In 1939 San Francisco decided to have a world's fair. It was a delightful one, even if small. It was all Southwestern adobe style, and the whole place was a village in that style. They didn't have these various monolithic or exaggerated machines and buildings. It was a very good fair, but it suffered in competition with New York.

Hallie sent me out to San Francisco to the world's fair of '39. The federal government had a very striking building. Inside that we were to build a Federal Theatre, which we did, with Izenour lighting. There were these huge rheostats on high crate boards, and each rheostat controlled a lamp. The electrician would be spreading himself over the whole board—standing on one foot, one arm out here, and one here, and a foot here—handling this rheostat.

There was this mad artist, George Izenour,[16] who thought that something should be done about it, so he developed the electronic switchboard, which he started with bulbs and tubes instead of chips to lower the lights or raise the lights. He went to Hallie, and with her always-open mind, she said, "Well, it's worth a try. Give this man a chance." So we let him develop the switchboard at Treasure Island [the manmade fair site in San Francisco Bay] in 1939, and it worked. Here was this madman sitting, moving little switches and getting all these effects. Yale was so impressed with it that they took him away from Federal Theatre and gave him a laboratory of his own.

I think a lot of the designers who came out of the Federal Theatre had as a useful part of their training that they had to work with minimals. If you couldn't give full scenery background, you used set pieces or lighting. I think that they learned a lot there perforce. There were a lot of people working in lighting. Abe Feder[17] was said to be the man who got the least light out of the most instruments [laughter].

I brought in five units from the coast, Federal Theatres from Seattle, San Francisco, Los Angeles, San Diego, and Portland, Oregon. One of them was a dance unit, one was a Living Newspaper unit, one of them did a children's show, one did contemporary comedy, and one did a classic. We alternated them. We had shows going all through the day and the evening and cut each one down to an hour, so anybody could have a taste of what Federal Theatre was doing all over the country.

One of my units at the Federal Theatre on Treasure Island was a wonderful Negro unit. I think it was from Seattle. They were doing Hall Johnson's opera, *Run, Little Chillun.*[18] The first act is all voodoo, and the second act is all religious shouting. And they were wonderful at it.

I had as the director for it Hall Johnson's assistant, a little man named Jaster Hairston. He was about so high, a little black man who is a great musician. Hall Johnson by that time was deep into drink, so Jaster had been running the choir. He came over and directed this *Run, Little Chillun* and had the most terrific energy. He was directing one of gospel-shouting scenes, and many of the Negro actors were not only college graduates, but there were M.A.s and even Ph.D.s among them. They had some hesitation about fitting the Negroid pattern, you know-the idea that all Negroes are good singers and dancers and shuffle along. He got up on a chair-he was only five feet tall-and he said, "Folks, let's get Negroid." And he got his results.

HALLIE FLANAGAN

Well, you're asking a prejudiced person [about Hallie Flanagan]. I thought she was wonderful. I saw very few flaws in Hallie. I thought particularly her ability with artists—being herself an artist—she knew how to bring out the best in them. I can't remember any time when I observed her telling an actor or a director or a playwright how to do it. Her method was a wonderful teaching method, drawing out the best in that person: "What would happen if . . . ?" Or "What do you think . . . ?" Or "Have you considered . . . ?"

Hopkins had tried several thoroughly professional, seasoned theatre people and had been turned down by them, which I think was fortunate for Federal Theatre, excepting I suppose somebody like Elmer Rice would have been useful with Congress. Certainly, Hallie was the ideal one for the job. Hopkins knew her from Grinnell.

Aside from that, she had what we might laughingly call ideals. She had a vision, which very few people had, of a national theatre. She had more patience than anybody I've ever known with fools and with incompetents. She knew theatre, not only just the Broadway style but regional and academic. She had a great deal of energy and belief as well as knowledge.

When it was created as a Federal Theatre, the attitude of the whole professional theatre was very dubious, from thinking it wasn't worth bothering with to being very much opposed to it. The unions, who were in the middle of that scale, were not helpful at all. The Federal Theatre was going to take in unemployed actors who had never reached Equity membership but who had a bio that showed that they had been actors. We observed Equity's rules, excepting for the fact that if a person had been on relief and could show that he had been in the theatre, he was taken in even though he wasn't Equity. They were sent to me, and I interviewed them as you would interview a candidate for casting, only I wanted some evidence of what they had done in theatre. When you're hungry, it's very easy to lie. I had a very hard time turning some down.

I think Hallie was an innocent politically. She did not recognize, as she should have, from the very start, as we all should have, her political responsibilities. She didn't recognize that before anything else, her job was to get Congress's goodwill, to cultivate the congressmen who would be necessary for the continuation of the project. She was too deeply involved in the work of establishing this terrific organization, and so [HUAC Chairman Martin] Dies[19] had his way.

I really never said goodbye to Hallie. Although I wasn't serious at that time, I was, I guess, personally almost in love with her, and I kept up with her. I went on to other things, and she went back to Poughkeepsie and to her husband, who was a very dear man. And then she lost him. We kept in correspondence, and I'd see her now and then.

This president of Smith College came over to Poughkeepsie and said to Hallie, "We need a new dean. Smith has never been great in theatre; we want to establish a theatre department." He'd been stupid enough not to consult his faculty at all, so he announced to his faculty that he had chosen the dean and the new head of a new department of theatre without consulting them at all.

I went with her as her assistant there and had a very rough row to hoe because we didn't know why there was such resentment, particularly in the English Department, which of course had all the theatre up to that time. So she had a very rough go of it. She turned Smith into coed, by the way. An innovation of hers at Smith, as it had been at Vassar, was bringing men in to play the men's parts in the girls' shows. She recruited the faculty and townsfolk to play the men's parts.

THE DIES COMMITTEE: "ANTICOMMUNISTS' MADNESS"

Congress was bullied by Dies. The primary thing was the anticommunists' madness. Dies managed to make the whole country think they saw Communists under every bed. Some of our best artists had to go abroad because they couldn't find work, and everybody bowed down to his bullying. That was certainly the major cause, because Congress was the means by which this government project could be continued—or not continued, as turned out to be the case.

Obviously, the unemployed were a great field for radical organizers, weren't they? We had to deal with the Independent Workers of the World—wasn't it?—IWW, who formed a very strong unit in the New York area.

The relief rolls were a good field for radical organizers, and we had a lot of problems with the Workers' Alliance versus Actors' Equity, but I don't feel that they ever achieved any power within the organization at all. Of course, it was illegal to ask anybody his politics in the first place. It was absolutely against the rules not only in Federal Theatre but also in the arts projects and in the whole WPA. You had no right to ask a man what his politics were, and it was a very serious offense to do so. Certainly, a lot of the men were left-wing sympathizers because the radicals offered what sounded like a solution. When we were all kids, we looked at the *Communist Manifesto* and said, "That's a great idea."

I think a lot of the administrators were certainly liberals, if I can use that dirty word now, and nowhere in the management of the administration did Communism have any real influence. I did an analysis for Hallie to present to Congress, which she was never allowed to do. I analyzed all of the plays that had ever been done on every Federal Theatre project. I was able to say that perhaps one percent of these plays might be called really radical and about another two percent might called socialist, left wing.

The rest were not. Most of them were Shakespeare, classics, successful Broadway plays, new plays about the region—for instance, in the Northwest about the settlers from Scandinavia. But of course, the troublemakers focused on the few things that gave them a slight foothold.

As in all projects, whether it's road building or Wall Street, there's always somebody who's not going to follow the rules. There was in Federal Theatre as in WPA. In New York it was murder because in the first place, you had to be careful about how many were Equity and non-Equity and the whole city budget, which included God knows how many different Units. There was plenty of red tape and paperwork. When I got to Washington, one of my assignments was analyzing the reports from the various units, particularly as the hearings developed.

In Hollywood, people couldn't get jobs if they were just mentioned by Mr. Dies, and had no opportunity to clear themselves. If they had, let's say, forty years ago joined the party because it had ideals, and had long since gone away from it, they were still tainted.

Sam Wanamaker went to London. Here is a man who was a fine actor, had a great concept of rebuilding the Globe Theatre, could have been an asset to the American Theatre. People like Paul Robeson, whom we lost, and in a country where supposedly you have free speech. As long as you aren't throwing bombs, you have a right to say what your politics are.

"WE *HAD* A NATIONAL THEATRE"

I think she was too busy making this thing come true to really think very much about its turning into a national theatre. For a nation like this, centralized theatre makes very little sense. To have a company in Washington or in New York which now and then goes out traveling into the field is not for us. It's for England, where in a couple of hours they can be at the borders of the country from the base in London. Here we're so diverse and so geographically dispersed that it's impossible to think of a national theatre for America.

In Europe, before it accumulated into the larger countries of France, Germany, Italy, it was a bunch of little duchies and dukedoms. The duke had his own army and his own post office and his own opera house. When it gathered together into France and Germany and Italy, it was the natural thing for the new government to take over the customs house and the military and the opera house. So, the citizens of Europe grew up with the arts. The Italian peasant plowing the field sings opera.

America, on the other hand, is cultivated by a group of pioneers who went out into the woods to shoot something for the table and to build a cabin. If you wanted entertainment, you plunked your guitar. As a result of that, several of the performing arts are mysteries.

In England in Shakespeare's time, there were four classes of people—thieves, rogues, vagabonds, and actors—who were beyond the protection of the law. [Others] could do anything [against them] they wanted to, and you had no redress at all. A certain amount of that feeling still persists, I think, in the far, back minds of the American public.

You have to have a certain skill with a paintbrush, or to get on your feet and dance, or to play an instrument, but you don't need anything to act. You can playact. You've been moving your legs and arms since you were born, and you've been talking since you were two. So there's no great respect for the theatre of all the performing arts.

We *had* a national theatre, by the way [the Federal Theatre]. If it had been allowed to continue, it would have developed into a nationally subsidized, permanent theatre, which would have been even more brilliant than it was.

The national theatre that Hallie envisioned, we have it right now. We have all sorts of wonderful regional theatres, the Long Wharf, the Hartford Stage, the Goodman in Chicago. You can name them, scores of first-class theatres doing fine work and frequently playing to their regions.

I think the regional, professional, and the academic, and the amateur community theatre groups also exist as an American national theatre. Michigan was the first of many who have professional theatre adjuncts. They're part of the University [of Michigan], which not only serves their community but serves their students and particularly their graduate students. We worked the best of the graduate students into the professional companies we brought in.

In community theatres there's plenty of amateur work that is just as good as professional. I had a year in Kalamazoo. You're really a trouper if you played Kalamazoo. I was director of the community theatre. The Johnson Chemical Company, I think, owns Kalamazoo [pharmaceutical giant Upjohn, now part of Pfizer, had its headquarters there], and they built a beautiful little, charming community theatre. They might have been gasoline station attendants or bank presidents or whatever, but on nights and weekends, they had bodies and souls that belonged to me, and we did some very serious and very good work.

Matter of fact, we did *The American Way*. It was the history of a German immigrant coming to America, growing up, and making his way in America. It's done with everything but elephants and camels. It had fifteen scenes, and we involved the whole town. The Ladies Aid made the costumes, and the Rotary Club did the lighting, and the Masons did the scenery. And we toured it around from Kalamazoo to several local places, also.

That kind of community theatre is the third branch of what I consider the coming American national theatre.

"I WANT HE SHOULD SAY HE SEEN SHAKESPEARE"

During Hallie's hearings, when it was so obvious that they weren't even going to let her make a statement about what we'd been doing, there was a story told that still brings tears to my eyes. We had a wagon stage going in the tur-pentine camps in Florida. We felt it was part of their job to bring theatre to the people. They'd get out to this wilderness in Florida, they'd drop the sides and the ends and make a stage. And they'd put on Shakespearean plays. One night there was an elderly man bringing a boy in, and the boy was about so big. The company manager said to this man, "Isn't he pretty young for Shakespeare?" And the old man said, "I want he should say he seen Shakespeare. I did once when I was a kid." Knocks me out.

❖   ❖   ❖

ROBERT SCHNITZER *(born 1906) is a former actor, producer, educator, and theatre administrator. From 1936 to 1939 he was Delaware's state director and deputy national director of the Federal Theatre Project. He joined ANTA as a general manager and later took over the International Exchange Program. Hundreds of overseas appearances arranged by Schnitzer ran the gamut from college choirs to Marian Anderson, the Dave Brubeck Quartet, and the New York Philharmonic under the direction of Leonard Bernstein. He later joined the American Repertory Company, set up the Theatre Guild, and during the 1970s headed the University of Michigan's Professional Theatre Program.*

PART 2 NOTES

[1]**Clifford Odets** (1906–1963) is considered the quintessential playwright of the 1930s. A member of the Group Theatre, he created a sensation on January 14, 1935, when his play *Waiting for Lefty* opened. Odets spoke not only for striking taxi drivers but for a dispossessed working class. The play incorporated the realistic "method" acting style nurtured by the Group. He later wrote *Awake and Sing!*, *Paradise Lost*, *Golden Boy*, *Rocket to the Moon*, and *Country Girl*.

[2]Along with Odets, **William Saroyan** (1908–1981) is considered one of the leading playwrights of the 1930s Depression era. Both the Group Theatre and the Theatre Guild produced his work. In 1939 he rejected the Pulitzer Prize for his play *The Time of Your Life* on the grounds that the award was materialistic.

[3]**Hallie Flanagan Davis,** nee Ferguson (1890–1969) was an academic before directing the Federal Theatre. After graduating from Grinnell (Iowa) College, she studied with George Pierce Baker at Harvard's Workshop 47, winning a Guggenheim in 1927. From her European travels, she brought back new techniques in the theatre to her experimental program at Vassar College. These would form the basis of many of the Federal Theatre Project's groundbreaking techniques in the theatre. In 1935 Harry Hopkins, the head of the Works Progress Administration under Franklin Roosevelt, invited her to become director of the WPA's Federal Theatre Project. Her dream of a "national theatre" was not to be realized, as the project tried to reconcile art

with a relief mission designed to put people to work. Despite the problems and its short life (1934–1939), the Federal Theatre Project period would contribute more to the American theatre than any other time in history.

[4]**Rose McClendon** (1884–1936) was appointed director of the Harlem Unit and chose John Houseman as her codirector. Her choice of a white director was based on her recognition of Houseman's skills and experience in the theatre and her wish to provide the best possible training for an underserved black population of actors, directors, and playwrights.

[5]**Orson Welles** (1915–1985) began his career at the Dublin's Gate Theatre in 1931. Shortly after, he toured with Katherine Cornell, making his debut in the New York theatre in *Romeo and Juliet.* A versatile actor, playwright, and director, Welles came to prominence in the Federal Theatre Project at the age of 20. He left to found the Mercury Theatre with John Houseman and later created a national panic with H.G. Wells's *War of the Worlds,* broadcast nationwide in 1938. Welles went on to a movie career, writing, directing, and acting in *Citizen Kane,* one of the most important films in American cinema.

[6]***The Tragical History of Doctor Faustus*** (1937) was conceived by John Houseman and Orson Welles, with Orson playing Faustus. It followed the Federal Theatre's dedication to classics as well as modern drama, but it was the ultimate magic show, with light effects, trapdoors, explosions, sound effects, and the Seven Deadly Sins played by puppets.

[7]**The House Un-American Activities Committee** (HUAC) would step up its hunt for Communists in the arts in the late 1940s and '50s. In 1952 the Senate permanent investigations subcommittee (Government Operations Committee) came under the chairmanship of Senator Joseph McCarthy (R-Wisconsin). Determined to weed out alleged communism in the country, these committees would again attack artists and the arts, leading the movie and theatre industries to devise blacklists of those who would not work again until many years later.

[8]Writers **Richard Wright, Ralph Ellison, Gwendolyn Brooks,** and **Margaret Walker** were among the leading voices of the writers of the Harlem Renaissance of the 1920s and '30s and part of the celebration of black cre-

ativity, modernism, liberation, sensuality, and hedonism in the literature, art, music, and dance of the period.

[9]**The Lafayette Theatre** in Harlem was the home of the largest of the Negro Theatre units, which presented thirty productions between 1935 and 1939.

[10]***The Trial of Dr. Beck*** (1938), written by Hughes Allison, portrayed the murder trial of a doctor accused of murdering his wife. It dealt not only with discrimination in the white community but with prejudice within the black community. Its mixed cast got a warm reception and unanimous raves from the press.

[11]**Madame C.J. Walker** (1867–1919) was born on a Louisiana plantation and went on to become one of the most successful black international business-women of the twentieth century. A political activist and philanthropist, she established a modern black hair care and cosmetics empire.

[12]***Conjur Man Dies*** (1936) was based on the novel *The Conjure-Man Dies: A Mystery Tale of Dark Harlem* by Harlem Renaissance writer and physician Rudolph Fisher. The book is considered the first black detective novel.

[13]**Theodore Ward** is best known for his play *Big White Fog* (1938). The main character is a follower of Marcus Garvey's ill-fated Back to Africa movement. The play was accused of being Communist propaganda, based on its theme of whites and blacks working together to fight oppression.

[14]***Haiti*** (1938) was written by William Du Bois, a reporter for the *New York Times* who had written a few melodramas for producer David Belasco. He based this play on the Haitian rebellion against France. The main character, Henri Christophe, led the struggle for independence for a black Haiti. Produced at the Lafayette Theatre in 1938, *Haiti* played to over seventy-seven thousand people. It toured to Boston and was also produced in Hartford, Connecticut.

[15]**Walter (Dougherty) Hampden** (1879–1955) was an actor-manager in the classic style. His career only began when he could finance the plays that would present him. In the 1920s and '30s, he brought Shakespeare to appreciative

audiences throughout America. He played Rostand's Cyrano de Bergerac more than a thousand times in fifteen years and Shylock in the *Merchant of Venice*.

[16]**George Izenour** (b. 1912), a theatre design and engineering consultant, invented the electronic console for stage lighting control, the synchronous winch system, and the steel acoustical shell. From November 1937 to December 1938, he supervised lighting for all Federal Theatres in Los Angeles.

[17]After leaving Chicago's Goodman Theatre, lighting designer **Abe Feder** (b. 1909) arrived in New York in 1930 and began lighting Yiddish theatre productions. He designed for Broadway as well as for the Federal Theatre. He became Orson Welles's technical director for the New York Federal Theatre. In Welles's *Doctor Faustus*, he brought characters on and off the stage by using pools, curtains, and walls of light, and nothing more.

[18]*Run, Little Chillun* (1939) was produced at the Golden Gate Exposition on Treasure Island in San Francisco Bay. It had played previously at the Alcazar Theatre in Los Angeles to audiences who were swept away by its scenes of tribal ritual, voodoo, and elemental beauty.

[19]**Martin Dies** (1890–1972) was a congressman from Texas who led the first House Un-American Activities investigation in the 1930s.

Hallie Flanagan with Sinclair Lewis, opening night, *It Can't Happen Here*, Adelphi Theatre, New York, 1936

"Voodoo" Macbeth, 1936

John Houseman with Orson Welles, 1936

Woodie King, Jr., New York, 2001

Conjur Man Dies, Lafayette Theatre, New York, 1936

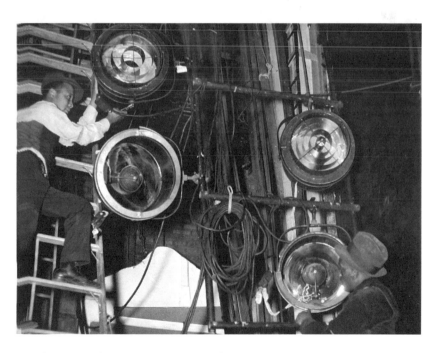

Lighting technicians, Negro Theatre Unit, New York, 1938

The Trial of Dr. Beck, New York, 1937

Robert Schnitzer, New York, 2001

Hallie Flanagan and Harry Hopkins, opening night at *Battle Hymn*, Biltmore Theatre, New York, 1936

Julius Caesar, directed by Orson Welles, Mercury Theatre production

San Francisco World's Fair, Treasure Island, 1939

George Izenour at lighting board, 1939

Run Little Chillun, Los Angeles, 1939

Hallie Flanagan testifying before the Dies Committee,
Washington, D.C., 1939

Stage wagon at Turpentine Camp, circa 1938

THE
WRITERS

ARTHUR MILLER

FEDERAL THEATRE
PLAYWRIGHTING DIVISION

I think they probably were responsible for the one big invention of the theatre in our time, which was the Living Newspaper. This was a real invention. There's been nothing like it that I know of since.

I had to go find a job, of course, and there weren't any, so I thought I'd get on one of the projects of the Federal Theatre. That wasn't so easy, because you had to be on welfare in order to get a job. I could still live at home in my parents' house; at least I had a roof over my head, but I didn't have any income. They insisted that you couldn't have a roof over your head at all even if you had no income. A friend of mine had a room over on Forty-something Street and Eighth Avenue. I moved in there. I had a pair of shoes there and a hat, and the inspector came to see whether I really lived there. He decided I did. So that's how I qualified for the project.

I got on what was then a new project: the playwriting division. It hadn't existed more than a month or two before I arrived, and it was still in a state of disorganization. Nobody knew quite what it was supposed to be doing. They had about twenty or thirty people on the project who weren't writers or playwrights, and none of us had ever had a production of any kind. It was a situation where people who were claiming to be playwrights or wanted to be playwrights were suddenly dubbed "playwrights." You can imagine that very little came out of it. As far as I know, there may have been one other man who was a playwright who continued to write plays.

In time it probably would have developed into something. It only lasted six or eight months, so it wasn't given enough time to mature. I was writing a tragedy about Montezuma and Cortez with about forty characters. If the project had lasted longer, it possibly could have been done because they had a lot of actors. It couldn't have been done commercially, for certain. It was the only place you could do a play like that. So it invited big ideas.

THE LIVING NEWSPAPER

The Federal Theatre, when it started out, was very exciting. I think they probably were responsible for the one big invention of the theatre in our time, which was the Living Newspaper. This was a real invention. There's been nothing like it that I know of since.

Basically, it was the dramatization of an issue. It could be the Triple-A program of the Agricultural Department, which was to plow under crops to keep the prices up while people were starving in cities. It could be about the absence of medical care in the cities. Could be about, God knows, any social public issue. We found a way of combining dramatic scenes—some of them comic, some of them serious—with the use of photographs, in a crude way of blowing them up. You had a big screen onstage, which was useful. It was a documentary kind of a thing, basically. One of the subjects was the electrification of the farms [Power]. Until 1932 only a small fraction of American farms had electricity.

As I recall, they used a lot of songs; there was use of popular music. It was unbelievable, the mélange of forms. Oh, anything went—they had vaudeville, they had dance.

It was also novel in the sense that no one writer wrote them. They were written really by a group, the way movies were written. It's precisely the same situation. They had an editor-producer, Arthur Arent, and they had different writers working on different scenes. It was a big collaborative thing.

The Living Newspaper audience was like the audience for the *Daily News*: The whole city was there. There were people from Park Avenue and people from Third Avenue and people from God knows where—partly, I suspect, because there were some good actors in it who were attractive, and also the cost of the theatre ticket was so low. Anybody who could go to a movie could go to the Federal Theatre, so it was terrific. That spirit was more important than anything, and I think ultimately that it survived. It's the kind of a spirit that would have generated a lot of work, because it was inviting. You got the feeling: Well, if I write something, then somebody will do it. Broadway, as you know, was always negative about any kind of a challenging form or work. For example, they did *Murder in the Cathedral*,[1] which could never have appeared in a commercial theatre at that time.

THE PLAYWRIGHTING DIVISION

My sense of it is that outside of New York, the level of production was kind of medium, because anybody could get on and say he's an actor. Consequently, I'm sure that a lot of it was not very good. Of course, there were a lot of very good actors involved in New York and probably in L.A. After all, if you put a play on in Dubuque, Iowa, you couldn't expect to get the level of acting that you would in the big cities, where the actors tend to congregate.

After my first couple of days there, I read one or two scenes from my colleagues. I felt that they weren't playwrights, and I was hardly in a position to say that, because I was just out of college. There's a certain tone that you get after a real page of dialogue, and I wasn't hearing it. Most of it was trivial, as usual, but you could make a living at it. After I got inoculated into Federal Theatre, I thought, Well, I'd better go somewhere else, 'cause I didn't feel that it was really, as yet, a serious place for playwrights. I think in time it could have become one. Let's suppose they had actually found a good script, which was conceivable among that group of writers. They produced it, and it was more or less interesting or successful. It would have started some kind of a motion, a movement, and good writers would have shown up, and productions would have happened, and you might have had a thing going. As it was, it was blown out of the water in a matter of months.

I don't know what I would have done without it. I regarded it as simply a way of keeping myself alive till I got some way of making a living. I probably would have left even if it had not exploded and vanished, because the big opportunity for playwrights in those days was radio. There were still a lot of radio shows that used real playwriting.

The Federal Theatre was a lifesaver for me, because in those few months after I got out of school, I really needed some quick work. Had it not been for that, I'm not sure what would have happened. As it was, I was able to spend my time writing. To be sure, it was writing something that nobody produced, but it was important to write it, anyway. From there I started writing radio. You got a hundred dollars for a script, but it was wonderful. There were no commercials on CBS national network.

I can't remember what the ticket price was, but it was pennies. The audience was really New York. There were all kinds of people: There were blacks, Hispanics—everybody was there. It's the first time and maybe the last time that I was conscious of the whole city being in the audience. And it was very touching, I thought.

They would have made it, had it not been censored to death. It was struggling to get out of the womb, the Federal Theatre, and it never quite made it, tell the truth. It never got its feet on the ground. It was attacked; it was ridiculed; it was finally simply obliterated.

It was usually the right wing who didn't want the government doing Federal Theatre. It thought the government should be absolutely out of what they called "the business." They shouldn't be regulating anything. It should be viewed as a government of perhaps observers at best but not participating in the life of the country. So, they were opposed to the whole New Deal, and the Federal Theatre was part of the New Deal.

The Federal Theatre also did children's plays, which of course don't exist anymore; in fact, this may be the only theatre in the world that has no children's theatre.

The production which finally closed down the whole Federal Theatre was *The Revolt of the Beavers,* which was written by a friend of mine, Oscar Saul, may he rest in peace. It was a children's play, and the kids adored it. They had these beavers who were being exploited by a bad beaver. The kids hated the old, bad beaver, and they loved these little, sweet beavers, and the little beavers were running all over the stage being persecuted by the capitalist beaver. Brouhaha started that this was Communist propaganda, which in a way I suppose it was, but I don't think it converted anybody or anything. Anyway, that was the excuse for closing it down. And so everybody went off to Hollywood.

SUBSIDIZED THEATRE

These things can't sustain themselves. They have to be subsidized, and we don't do that. The difference between the commercial theatre and the

Federal Theatre was that the commercial theatre was essentially an entertainment for as broad a middle-class audience as they could manage to sell tickets to. The Federal Theatre was trying to move to the edge of the theatre, and some of their productions were in fact inventions as far as theatre is concerned, new ways to tell stories. Such a thing was not possible in the commercial theatre because it involved a lot of people, large casts, usually music, and a radical viewpoint, more or less, toward society, toward life, which would have shocked some of the orchestra tickets.

A commercial theatre is always loath to take risks, not only here but in France and Germany and England. You know, Bernard Shaw had to work for seven years to get a play by Ibsen produced in London, and he could only do it when he got some very heavy stars to play it for three or four weeks. This is an old story. There grew up post–World War II, in England certainly and to a degree in France, a noncommercial, subsidized theatre that took risks and tried to move to the edge in terms of production. They didn't have to make any money. There have been subsidized theatres in Europe since two hundred years or more, but not quite like this. This was an attempt really to engage the whole population in the theatre.

I think it's perfectly obvious that the basic organization of those British theatres springs out of the Federal Theatre. Hallie Flanagan invented a way of doing this. Now, the difference is that with us you had to be on welfare. This was basically a way of keeping actors and other theatre people from starvation. A lot of talented people couldn't participate, because they weren't broke. They had some financial means, and you weren't allowed to have any. That was a big limitation.

I got twenty-two dollars and seventy-seven cents a week. That was my pay. Normally, I maybe would have gotten that just to keep from falling to pieces. This way I had to work. All these actors were performing. They were doing something for the money that they were getting and very happily doing so. So, the government got a bargain.

Furthermore, a lot of these actors—or a number of them, anyway—went on to become very heavy taxpayers. I think between four or five of those people, they probably paid the cost of the whole Federal Theatre back in the next fifteen years. I'm not exaggerating. Their income tax probably paid for the whole damn thing. It's really incredible. So even from the business point of view, it made good sense.

A lot of theatres were dark then, and when you've got a theatre that's working, all the surrounding businesses prosper—I mean the hotels and restaurants and the rest of 'em, taxis. If you add all that up, the government got a terrific bargain because all those people pay taxes who are benefiting from the theatre. The government got off really well.

The positive side of it far outweighs the negative, because it makes it possible to do stuff in the theatre that's thrilling. It involves the community in the theatre. It involves the society in the theatre. Instead of this peanut stand that we run here on five blocks on Broadway which makes multimillionaires out of a handful of people, we could have some kind of a real engagement with society in the theatre, and that would be great.

There's an old tradition in America that if you can't get it to pay, it's not worth anything. Now we're even privatizing Social Security—I mean, they'll privatize death soon. You can't think in terms of a social duty or obligation or an opportunity. Everything is private.

At the moment the government gives a pittance to the arts, and all over the United States, theatres are closing, or they're in bad shape, or they're desperate, or they are not doing the stuff they want to. They do popular stuff in order to get some kind of an income from the box office. In England when they come in and sit down, or in Sweden or in France, the people come in. It's their theatre. It doesn't belong to the Shuberts; it belongs to them, and they're very warm about it and very proud when it does something wonderful. It's a great thing. It's a great socializing process. Makes people feel part of the society instead of alienated from it.

What killed it is the first lifting of the Depression and a new attitude toward the world as a result of the oncoming World War II, which made people feel that the important thing was going to be this conflict. Something happened in the American psyche. It's hard to describe. I found there was less interest in anything but survival. There was antifascism. There was pro-fascism. There was neutrality. There was a real battle going on in the minds of the American people at that time, and theatre couldn't keep up with that, I don't think. Then there was, of course, the success of the anti–New Deal ideology. Roosevelt was being edged off the stage at that moment.

The accusations against Federal Theatre that it was propaganda were partly that. It was propaganda generally for the liberal ideology. At the same time they were doing T.S. Eliot,[2] who was on the far right, they were also doing *It Can't Happen Here*,[3] which was the antifascist American work by Sinclair Lewis. Probably because they had a dozen companies doing that play all over the United States, that may have done more than anything else to turn on that light that this was basically a propaganda tool. You know, one man's truth is another man's propaganda. O'Neill didn't write any conservative plays. O'Neill was basically a socialist himself, and if you want to interpret his plays politically, they were on the left. I think they were complaining that there were no right-wing playwrights. That was not the Federal Theatre's fault. They just weren't around.

THEATRE IN TODAY'S SOCIETY

The role of theatre in America today is basically one of entertainment. That's why people go. It's probably why they always went, but the question is, What is entertaining? If you want the most trivial kind of entertainment, that's one thing. If you want something more profound, meaningful, it's harder to write, harder to do good, harder to act. If you just want to please the crowd, it's a lot easier.

Our problem now is that it's big in New York, it's so totally commercialized, that most young writers don't even try to become playwrights. If they do, it's simply as a way to the movies and television. As Bob Anderson said, "You can make a killing, but you can't make a living." It's totally in the lap of landlords and people who want to make the buck. The spirit of it is the spirit of real estate, which is not very conducive to creative work.

There's a lot of good work being done in the United States, but it never gets to Broadway. The musicals get to Broadway—which, of course, some of them are terrific—but the straight play doesn't, because it can't compete with a musical. A musical doesn't have to be great to be good. It can just tap your feet, and it's good enough. For a play to run a long time, or a reasonable time, is much more difficult. I've had plays just taken off the stage in the last three, four years—that were making money—because they figured they can make more money with a musical or with a big hit from London. So it's tough.

And that's my word for today.

❖   ❖   ❖

ARTHUR MILLER *is considered America's greatest living play-wright. Born in New York City and educated at the University of Michigan, he began his career as a script reader as part of the Federal Theatre's Playwrighting Bureau. His play* Death of a Salesman (1949) *won him both the Pulitzer Prize and the Drama Critics' Circle Award.* The Crucible (1955), *a drama of the Salem witchcraft trials written in response to Senator Joseph McCarthy's investigations of accused subversives, continues to be performed as a contemporary parable. His many other plays include* All My Sons (1947), A View from the Bridge (1955), After the Fall (1964), The Price (1968), *and* The Ride Down Mount Morgan (1994). *Recent works include his memoirs,* Timebends: A Life, *and* Echoes down the Corridor: Collected Essays, 1944–2000.

PART 3 NOTES

[1]*Murder in the Cathedral* (1935) had been rejected by the distinguished Theatre Guild Company. During its six-week Federal Theatre run, over thirty-nine thousand people saw the play. *Billboard* reported that "a hard-boiled audience of Broadway professionals stood up and cheered."

[2]**Thomas Sterns Eliot** (1888–1965) had seen Hallie Flanagan's production of his play *Sweeney Agonistes* at the Vassar Experimental Theatre. When Hallie met with him in England, he promised her another play about Thomas à Becket, the twelfth-century archbishop of Canterbury and martyr. That play, *Murder in the Cathedral*, became one of the first successes of the Federal Theatre.

[3]*It Can't Happen Here,* based on the book by novelist Sinclair Lewis, was created by Lewis, playwright Jack Moffitt, and a committee of theatre people working across the country. Hallie Flanagan described it as being "produced by polygenesis." After constant revisions the play opened on October 26, 1937, in twenty-one theatres in seventeen states. It was done in English, Spanish, and Yiddish. It was accused of being pro–Roosevelt New Deal, communist, fascist, and "PROPAGANDA—naked and unconcealed."

Arthur Miller, New York, 2001

Arthur Miller, circa 1939

Murder in the Cathedral, New York, 1936

Federal Theatre writers, circa 1935

Arthur Arent, writer, Living Newspaper Unit, New York

THE
VARIETY
ARTISTS

BOB BAKER

MARIONETTE UNIT, LOS ANGELES

*It was terrible. I wanted to go there; I wanted to go in there and rescue
some of the stuff, but I didn't dare. I was just a little kid. We were all
pretty quiet about it; and not only that: No one knew about it. When they
got rid of the Federal Theatre, there was a thing in the paper:
"Theatre Dies." So what?*

I don't think the Congress really liked the Federal Theatre. I don't think
the government liked it. They felt it was wasting money. That was always
my opinion. I think I wrote five letters to different congressmen asking
about the Federal Theatre, and their great remarks were, "Don't you know it
died in 1939? We felt it wasn't worth funding." I said, "Where are the
archives?" They said, "There's no such thing as archives of the Federal
Theatre."

THEATRE OF THE MAGIC STRINGS, LOS ANGELES

I was eight years old when I gave my very first puppet show, *Fiddler of Little
LeRoy*. I got paid fifteen dollars and figured this was a good profession to be
in, especially since it was Depression time. Some people didn't make that in
a whole week.

In the meantime, my Dad decided I should have a *Saturday Post* route and
learn how to handle money. We were delivering the *Post* early one morning
and coming around onto Wilshire Boulevard; I saw a puppet in a window. I
asked my father to stop the car, and we took a look. This was going to be the

future home of the Federal Theatre's Theatre of the Magic Strings. I said to my dad, "I want to work there." My dad said, "You can't. First of all, I make a very fine salary; we're not on relief. You have to be on relief to work in the WPA. Just forget it."

The next day at school, I met a young man whose family was on relief. He was an NYA, National Youth Authority. He says, "Why don't you tell 'em you're twelve years old?" I was nine or ten. "Tell 'em that you want to be in the NYA and you want to work at the puppet theatre."

So, one day I roughed up my clothes, and I went in. I don't think I used the word "destitute," but I said we needed help and we needed money and I would like to work under NYA and be in the puppet theatre. The man who was in charge at that time, Mr. Bob Bromley, says, "Okay, you can work here." So I went to work.

The first day the checks came out, I got very worried. I went to him and said, "Mr. Bromley, I can't work here." "Why not?" he says. "Well, first of all, I'm not twelve years old." "We know that," he said.

"You know, my family's not destitute, either." "We know that," he said.

"Well, I guess I just can't work here, can I?" And he said, "We didn't hire you. We said you could work here." And that's how I happened to be working in the Federal Theatre. I didn't get anything on the programs, and my name isn't listed anywhere.

I went there after school, gave them whatever time I had on Saturdays and Sundays when they did the shows. I finally got to the point where I was working up on the bridge. I was very proud of being looked at. I felt kind of extra special. I was rubbing shoulders with people who were professional puppeteers. I was getting a real introduction into the theatre. This was special. These were puppeteers.

The Puppeteers of America were kind of upset that [the FTP was] hiring people that didn't know anything about it. Some were artists that didn't want to adapt. There were two phases of puppetry: One is the artist who does the beautiful puppets, and the story is lost; or you have the actor who does these gorgeous readings and so forth, and the scenery is lousy.

I would sand their stuff, and I'd help paint. I was doing various things plus putting together the things that were going to be in the show, checking the strings. In those days we used very long, black lines, and we had to go up and down with our fingers to see if the lines had broken. If they had, we'd have to replace them. It wasn't until a few years later we started tying knots all over the place.

All of our shows were recorded. We would go across the street to the Music Project and record the show. They were on big acid tapes. The music would be all recorded there, too.

The first show was *Don Quixote*. That was the evening show. The afternoon shows were *Treasure Island* and *Crock of Gold*. In the evening they did marionette varieties, which was kind of a fun thing.

Disney came to the show when we did a thing called *Sweet Rumba*. We had a Leopold Stokowski puppet on a podium out front, and we had a process screen in the back. We'd do shadows of the orchestra moving in and out. It was a very beautiful thing. Walt was getting ideas for *Fantasia*, and he wanted the musicians and the artists to see what was going on there. He also was interested in what the puppets were doing.

We did a great thing from Poe, *The Raven*, a very stylized setting. Another was done to Stravinsky ballet music with very big puppets. These puppets were large and gorgeous things. I remember the finale, with all the confetti coming down on the stage and the lights changing.

YASHA FRANK, THE FAIR-HAIRED BOY

About that time, they got ready to move from the Theatre of the Magic Strings. Yasha Frank[1] was moving the Children's Theatre from the Beaux Arts down to the Mayan Theatre to do *Aladdin*. They needed a big stage 'cause they had flying carpets, all kinds of stuff going on, and big, big casts. We were to take over the theatre.

I've always thought that Yasha Frank was in the right place at the right time. He had a lot of doors opened for him by Hallie Flanagan. She wanted a good children's theatre, and he was able to come up with some very interesting shows. He was toted around by Hallie Flanagan. She always had him under tow and would take him around as the fair-haired boy of the whole project.

I loved his *Hansel and Gretel*.[2] I thought it was very revolutionary. He starts out with Mother Goose telling the story. Father Goose walks in, and he says, "You've got it all wrong. This is the way the story really goes," and from there, you go into the story. Down the aisle comes a horse. Hansel's on the horse, Gretel's onstage with the dog, and they play it for all it's worth.

Yasha brought in *Uncle Tom's Cabin*.[3] Lewis Carroll's *Alice in Wonderland*[4] was done. The only trouble about the Beaux Arts: It was a "long drink of water." It had been used for radio productions and chamber orchestras. It was fine for Yasha Frank's things, because the audience got very rowdy. They yelled and screamed and jumped up and down and tore up everything but the seats.

I watched *Pinocchio*.[5] He made it work. He did have magic. I was very unhappy when they did *Pinocchio* on television as a special and it wasn't very good. I heard that Yasha died a few months after that. Everybody said he committed suicide because that show was so bad.

They were fun shows. It wasn't a short time after that it was all gone.

CALIFORNIA FEDERAL THEATRE: PAGEANTS AND SPECTACLE

People love to see a spectacle. They love to see a pageant. If they have the backlog of people who are waiting to be in a production on the federal payroll, they can use them. They would borrow from other divisions. They would borrow from the Music Division and the Art Division if they needed somebody. Sometimes they didn't have the talent. An artist may not be an actor, and an actor may not be an artist, but by having these bigger pageants, they were able to advertise it as being the biggest, the most spectacular. In San Francisco I saw *The Winning of the West*. The trains moved in, and the people, the lighting, and the scenery were coming up from the floor. It was an amazing production. All those cavalcades that were being done for statehood and the finding of gold and Pony Express, I think those were all federally funded. I don't think anybody had that kind of money to put in shows like that at the time.

I know that people who had never been in a theatre went to see these shows. Everything became so real. Both in live theatre and puppet theatre, they would ask me, "Can you take me again? May I go again? May I go with you? Can I see another show?" There is something that's small and intimate. The most important, I think, is being able to get children into the theatre at an early age; then they'll always be a theatregoing person.

Most everything I saw as a young boy at the Theatre of the Magic Strings, at the Beaux Arts, the Mayan, the Mason Opera House, and the Hollywood

Playhouse, those were great, great experiences. You got a little booklet about so big, and it had a bunch of little pieces of paper. You'd tear out one of these things, and you'd have about a half a dozen more and put them in your pocket. You'd pay ten cents to go in and see a show. Nothing has ever been like that.

THE BONFIRE OF THE PUPPETS

On Western Avenue at Venice Boulevard was an old school called the Harvard School for Boys. It had been a military school since the early 1900s. The government took over this whole thing, including the playground and the athletic field, and had everything brought over there. They brought the scenery, the props, the grand pianos, the costumes, the puppets—every-thing—took 'em out on the field and burned them. They had desks and type-writers and wheelbarrows full of stuff that they just dumped out there in a big bonfire.

Well, the fire went for a long time. I watched it for a while. It was terri-ble. I wanted to go there; I wanted to go in there and rescue some of the stuff, but I didn't dare. I was just a little kid. We were all pretty quiet about it; and not only that: No one knew about it. When they got rid of the Federal Theatre, there was a thing in the paper: "Theatre Dies." So what?

❖ ❖ ❖

The BOB BAKER *Marionettes have entertained thousands of children and adults worldwide over the years. While attending Hollywood High School, Bob began manufacturing toy marionettes that sold in both Europe and the United States. After graduation he began his extensive career in animation at the George Pal Studios. He went on to become an animation advisor at many film studios, including Disney. His company still performs in a renovated scenic shop near downtown Los Angeles, where he builds marionettes for Disney.*

KATHERINE DUNHAM

FEDERAL THEATRE DANCE UNIT, CHICAGO

It wasn't until Southland, *a lynching ballet, that I got my fingers rapped by the State Department. It wasn't until then that I did something that I would say would be labeled as a serious, politically active thing. That's the sort of thing I did: just constantly interweave the racial context of society.*

I grew up near Chicago, in Glen Ellyn, Illinois. At that time it was just a very small kind of retreat for people who couldn't stand Chicago, which even then was a big, noisy, smoky place. When my mother died, we went from Glen Ellyn to Chicago. I lived with relatives on my mother's side, on the very fair, practically white side, and then after a while my father's relatives took us, so my life was back and forth. We went to Joliet, Illinois. I stayed there from the age of maybe seven until eighteen. And at that time, I went to Chicago and entered the University [of Chicago]. I had two years in junior college in Joliet.

I didn't know what I was going to do. I wanted to dance. I had that feeling all my life. If I'd hear music, I'd be out there doing something—I didn't know what.

Then I think my life really opened in a fashion that I would never have dreamed. I began seeing those things that I just had no idea existed, like anthropology, for instance. I had to get ready to major in something, and I didn't know what it would be. I said, "You know, I wish it could be in dance, but they don't have anything that would give me a major in that. I really don't know what to do." I was almost in tears.

My brother said, "Well, look—I've heard that you like anthropology. Go ahead, then; let that be your major." Just that year the university decided to honor anthropology and sociology by letting them become legitimate studies. I went to Dr. Redfield, who was one of the important men in anthropology. He was an acculturationist and helped me a great deal when I went to the West Indies. The idea of two cultures meeting was fascinating to me.

BALLET FEDRE: THE FEDERAL THEATRE DANCE UNIT IN CHICAGO

After I'd come back from the West Indies and gone back to school to get my master's degree, I went downtown in Chicago, wherever you had to go, and said I wanted to work. The WPA offices took my credentials.[6] Dozens of people were saying, "Give this woman a job." I had done a little writing, and I had my first book, called *Journey to Accompong*,[7] about a period of maybe thirty days spent with tribal Jamaican slaves who had managed to get free from their masters and had formed a unit. I went to see them, and I stayed with them.

Practically everything I did was unusual, so that I know now I am a catalyst. I don't think of myself as a dancer; I did what I had to do, what had to be done, and that's it.

I had to face the fact that I did not have one penny left from my fellowship, 'cause I got back to Chicago by some sort of—I don't know; I started to say "voodoo." I had a lot of company, so many, many people who had been students in the 1930s. It was a tough, tough period. That's why I feel extremely grateful for the WPA.

I think my parents would have disowned me if I had asked for welfare. They would rather go without a crust of bread than ask for welfare. You just didn't do it, so I had to make a decision then. I had no problem with tuition, because I had scholarships, but when it comes to just plain how do you make it, how do you live every day, and your carfare and that sort of thing—those things began to run out for me and for a lot of other people.

L'AG'YA

I wanted to take the dancing of black people and primitive peoples from all over the world and bring it to the American stage with so much authenticity that it wouldn't jar people.

L'Ag'Ya was a name of a fighting dance in Martinique. I did a little story that went with it and then the ballet.[8] It gave me an opportunity to stage and use John Pratt's costumes and present a full ballet. I would never in the world have been able to do that, you know. The costs for me would have been impossible.

They allowed me to hold auditions and pick out the people that I thought would be good for what I was doing. Where would I find people to do classical ballet, for instance? They weren't there; they didn't exist. I had to train them, and that was my particular gift. It's no good catalyzing and then leave somebody sitting there. I had to go and pick out people who had been—you name it—mechanics. I took them, and I made them into village people, and they loved it. I said, "Look, you don't carry your basket that way. Put it on your head." It was divine. Everything in it was the best. You had time to rehearse, time to work. The designers had time to get things done, and it was good theatre.

Another thing that the WPA could do: It could take things that had not been done before, ideas that had not been put in front of people. I'm forever grateful to the WPA for allowing me to do this ballet, which was very successful and which stayed with our repertoire for years and years. I'd still do it if the occasion presented itself. I'd do it tomorrow. It was great.

By this time I had met John Pratt, who became my husband, and we had a wonderful marriage of forty-nine years. John Pratt was a designer, and he designed The "Swing" Mikado. I did some dances for it. I had a line of men who had umbrellas hung over their arms, sort of British fashion, and tailcoats. It was really very amusing.

I moved to the Writers' Project. Most the time it would be articles that I would do. I'd already done two articles for Esquire magazine, under the name of K. Dunn because they were not publishing women at the time. It must have been 1936.

You know, this whole racism thing, it never came up. I think it was that they had no black students and no black teachers. They didn't think about it, but I had to think about it. I was teaching a combination of what I had learned in the West Indies and what, I guess, came through my own creative abilities. The fact that a black performer could get a dignified and demanding role in theatre and be recognized, I think that was extremely important. I'd say that this was an extremely important part of the evolution of black musicians, artists, and theatre artists.

I will tell you this: I feel that after the WPA closed and left us, that there was an effort to take this where it should have been going, you know, onward and upward. I don't think it's happened. I think that some of the great enthusiasm for good theatre and training and so forth and so on has been lost because there is no way to further it or develop it. I think it's a great loss, and so far I've not seen anything that would replace it.

If I think of the WPA, I can't understand why it is not in existence today. If ever anything was needed, that is needed. Somehow people don't seem to understand that the creative artist cannot always take care of his just plain subsistence needs, and that's been the problem with me and my company.

"ARE WE IN THE RIGHT GOVERNMENT, OR WHAT?"

Between the WPA and the ILGWU [International Ladies' Garment Workers' Union], I think I had my first serious feelings about political activism. Maybe I'd have lunch with Elia Kazan or maybe just talk—it was just the atmosphere. During the thirties, when it was a terrible thing of people not having enough to eat and all that kind of thing—I mean, real depression, economic depression—I think that it was only natural that people began to worry, "Are we in the right government, or what?" I don't think most of the people in the WPA, the performers, understood political activism, but I think that most of the directors and heads of projects did.

One of the things about the WPA was it gave some dignity to social activism. Let's face it: The WPA was making people understand more about themselves but also more about the relationship between the economic and the political crises that occur in any country. By giving money, food, or something, you can get people out of a tough spot, but if you don't go on and show them what to do next, you might as well just leave it alone. That's the thing I liked about the WPA. It helped to know what to do with your life, and that's what we lack.

I don't think enough came out of it in terms of political activism. I went to Europe and stayed there for years. It wasn't until *Southland*, a lynching ballet, that I got my fingers rapped by the State Department. It wasn't until then that I did something that I would say would be labeled as a serious, politically active thing. That's the sort of thing I did: just constantly interweave the racial context of society.

I think that there is a kind of thing where everything in your body will respond to outside influences, sounds, and sights. You can look at a wonderful thing that makes you feel that you want to move, or you can listen. That's my life. I've listened, and these things have given me motion.

❖   ❖   ❖

As early as the 1930s, KATHERINE DUNHAM *(born 1909) produced groundbreaking forms of dance by blending traditional dance with cultural anthropology. She studied native dance in the Caribbean in 1935, absorbing the sacred dance rituals of Haiti and Jamaica. As dance director of the Negro Unit of the Federal Theatre Project in Chicago, she choreographed dances for* Emperor Jones *and* Run, Little Chillun. *After the Federal Theatre, Dunham would go on to become one of the foremost choreographers in the country, with such credits as the Broadway musicals* Pins and Needles *and* Cabin in the Sky *and the operas* Aida *and* Faust. *The Dunham School of Dance, founded in the 1940s, still performs throughout the country.*

VIRGINIA WREN

FEDERAL THEATRE CIRCUS AND VAUDEVILLE UNITS, BOSTON

*When you came to a small town, you know, the circus was very exciting—
a lot of children and a lot of families. We had a great audience, and we
were special. We were big time!*

Vaudeville had died, and there was no work for people who had been
in the theatre. I guess when the Federal Theatre came along, people
were delighted that they could be employed at doing something that
they had done very well years before.

My sister and I and another young man did a club act. I played piano and
sang. I don't know how you would describe a "club"—not a speakeasy.
Different organizations wanted entertainment, and so we entertained them.

My husband did a wonderful, classy dance act called Cassidy, Cal, and
Baker, and it was quite elegant. They played the Boston area and even the
Palace Theatre in New York, which is the ultimate. He really had the background of show business. They used to call me "the First of May," which
meant a newcomer.

I guess I was a ham from the very beginning. In school I always played
piano from the time I was eight years old. I met my future husband in a
rehearsal hall in Boston, and they asked him if he could teach me a dance
act, tap dancing or hoofing. I didn't really know him, but he was very good-
looking and very nice and very charming. He said, "Could you learn a rou-
tine in a couple of weeks?" Of course I could, naturally—being very young,

you know, and full of confidence. In two weeks we had really quite a nice dance act. He was a wonderful dancer but also a wonderful teacher.

THE FEDERAL THEATRE VAUDEVILLE UNIT

I had heard that there was a Federal Theatre and that they were looking for people who had some background in theatre or vaudeville. So, I boldly went up and told 'em what I did. Everyone's kind of cute when you're seventeen, and they liked what I did. I remember thinking, What was I going to wear? There was a place called Filene's Basement where I got a black satin top that cost forty-seven cents and white flannel trousers that cost a dollar, and that was my outfit. We looked really quite elegant.

It was a wonderful time, but it was a tough time in many ways, because it was the end of the Depression. The sixteen dollars a week meant a great deal to me at that time. I gave my mother ten dollars a week and kept six dollars for myself. It was a great lesson because I had a very privileged childhood. I could do with little and appreciate what I had. I remember there was a little drugstore that had a lunch counter. Almost every day when we had a rehearsal, we'd go there. In this little place they made the most wonderful cream-cheese-and-black-olive sandwiches, and they were this thick. It may have been twenty-five cents or so with a cup of coffee. Those were great times, learning times. It taught me a very valuable lesson.

During the winter we played CCC camps, Civilian Conservation Corps, that employed young men cleaning up the forest and that sort of thing. Sometimes we'd play on the platform. Sometimes we played indoors, and they also fed us. We had a very enthusiastic audience. No wonder: They were desperate for some kind of entertainment. So, I guess we went over big.

We played hospitals—anyplace where they needed vaudeville.

It would take an hour for us to go up the Berkshires. Sometimes we didn't get home till one or two in the morning. Then I had to get on an elevated, 'cause we lived outside of Boston proper, then from there a streetcar, and then into my little tower. Mother always stayed up late and said, "Virginia, where are you?" "I'm here."

I can't imagine doing that today. I mean, I'd be dead. They liked us because we were sort of their age, and you know we were big time. We were sort of pre-USO, if you will. The women made sixteen dollars a week, and the men got twenty-three dollars a week. If you please, it still stands that men always get more.

FEDERAL THEATRE CIRCUS UNIT

In the summertime they got a big tent together. There were no animal acts, but there were different acts. We did what they call a flying ladder act. They said we're going to learn between two trees. They put a ladder between two trees and said, "There's nothing to it." I had the loop on my foot; then they said, "Now the next step will be you go backwards." I said, "Ohhh, I can't do that." They said, "We'll be right back here to hold you in case anything happens." And of course I did it, and they weren't there.

There were five girls around the wing, and a young man was attached to each girl because the ladder was too high for us to reach. The young man below had a rope and was pulling so that we were going up into the air. It was wonderful. It was very exhilarating. We did it in unison, and we had a wonderful circus band. They had a regular crew to set us up. We played Cohasset and many of the towns in New England up into the Berkshires.

One car drove one or two acts together, so they had a quite a number of drivers. It was a lot of work to put up a tent and then take it down again, because we were only there for one performance. There was a matinee and an evening performance, and that was it.

There were three sisters who had a bicycle act, doing all kinds of stunts on bicycles. They truly stood out 'cause they were old, honey: They were in their thirties; they were ancient. But, honey, when they'd get on those bikes, they really performed.

There was a man named Horace Greeley McKnabb who was a publicity agent, and he was dying to do a full-length story about yours truly. My family was quite shocked because he did a two-page spread in the now-defunct *Boston Traveler*. When he said that I came from a well-known circus family, I was persona non grata after that. In Europe, if you belong to a circus family, you were nobility, but in this country it's the lowest form of show business. I didn't think about it then, because we were having such fun.

My mother came to a matinee. I think she was stunned. She said, "How could you?" I said, "But Mom, it's such fun!" I was a sort of a rebel but in a quiet kind of way. And don't forget I was getting sixteen dollars a week.

When you came to a small town, you know, the circus was very exciting—a lot of children and a lot of families. We had a great audience, and we
were special. We were big time!

This is very embarrassing to me, because I've never spoken about it
before. When I say Federal Theatre, I didn't mention that "Federal" meant
government, but it was a challenge for us, because many other people were in
the same boat; many other people who had been making great salaries now
found that they had to accept a check from the government. But you know,
that's life, isn't it? That's life.

My husband and I finally got married, and the federal government didn't
like that, so they fired us. You can't be married and have two checks coming
in, if you please. With two checks coming to the same address, that was it,
they knew. So, goodbye, Charlie [laughs]!

❖   ❖   ❖

VIRGINIA WREN *lives in Connecticut, where she hosts a local
television show. She still plays piano and can still touch her toes.*

PART 4 NOTES

[1]**Yasha Frank,** director of the Children's Unit of the Federal Theatre in Los Angeles, had received a Ph.D. in psychology from New York University. He worked at MGM Studios under King Vidor, Erich von Stroheim, and Joseph von Sternberg. He also worked at the Chaplin and Pathé Studios. He resigned from Paramount Pictures to become director of the Children's Unit, which he called "the chance of a lifetime." He was also head of the Foreign Language Department of the Federal Theatre Project, producing plays in French, Yiddish, and Spanish.

[2]*Hansel and Gretel* (1937) was based on the opera by Humperdinck, as adapted by Yasha Frank.

[3]*Uncle Tom's Cabin* (1936) had an all-black cast and orchestra, which toured CCC camps and veterans' hospitals in New York state.

[4]*Alice in Wonderland* (1937) was directed by Ralph Chesse for the unit in Portland, Oregon.

[5]*Pinocchio* (1937), adapted by Yasha Frank, played to fifteen hundred children in a week's time.

[6]*Ballet Fedre,* created by Berta Ochsner, Grace and Kurt Graff, and Katherine Dunham, was performed under the auspices of the Chicago Federal Theatre Project. These choreographers, along with Ruth Page and Bentley

Stone, created works based on topical events and social problems. They choreographed such FTP productions as *The "Swing" Mikado* and *O Say Can You Sing*.

[7]***Journey to Accompong*** (1946) is Katherine Dunham's book based on her work as an anthropologist in the Caribbean, where she became an initiate of the voodoo religion and immersed herself in the language and culture, which later became the basis of her dance drama.

[8]***L'Ag'Ya*** (1937) is a seminal work displaying Dunham's blend of African-Caribbean influence and dance drama. Choreographed for the Chicago Federal Dance Unit, it was based on the folk life of Martinique.

Bob Baker, Los Angeles, 2000

Don Quixote, Los Angeles, 1936

Leopold Stokowski puppet, Los Angeles, 1936

Yasha Frank with Eddie Cantor at the Theatre of the Magic
Strings, Los Angeles

Alice in Wonderland, Seattle, 1938

Pinocchio, Los Angeles, 1937

Hansel and Gretel, Los Angeles, 1938

Katherine Dunham, New York, 2000

Katherine Dunham in *L'Ag'Ya*, Chicago, 1938

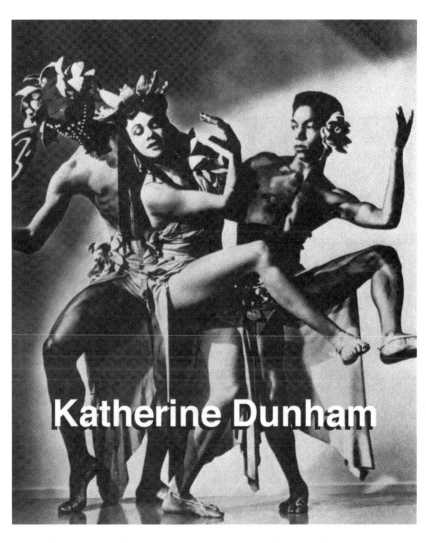

Katherine Dunham in *Primitive Rhythms*, Chicago, 1938

Virginia Wren, Connecticut, 2000

Federal Theatre Circus Unit, Boston

Federal Theatre Circus, putting up the "Big Top"

Federal Theatre Vaudeville Unit

OTHER
VOICES

CLINTON TURNER DAVIS

DIRECTOR, *CONJUR MAN DIES* RE-CREATION

NEW FEDERAL THEATRE, NEW YORK

One of the major legacies of the Federal Theatre Project and the Negro Units of the Federal Theatre Project was that it offered tremendous employment opportunities for African-American artists, gave voice to these artists, and made possible the growth that we have seen since the demise of the WPA.

Conjur Man Dies is considered by many to be the first African-American detective novel. This play is the precursor to the works of Ishmael Reed or Walter Moseley in terms of the African-American detective. The play was originally produced in 1936 at the Lafayette Theatre in Harlem as a part of the Negro Theatre Unit of the Federal Theatre Project. In *Conjur Man Dies*, as with all of the Negro theatre plays that were presented by the Negro Theatre Unit, there were whites involved in various aspects.

The characters that Rudolph Fisher[1] created in *Conjur Man Dies* are drawn from fantastic images of a wonderful cross section of people in Harlem. From Doctor Archer through the whole gamut of the upper classes to the lower classes, the people that one would normally see on the street: entertainers, numbers runners, types of professionals, as well as the very educated

class of people. With the novel, as well as in the play, to have all of these people onstage and interacting with each other was a phenomenal feat, particularly in its time, the 1930s.

The Bubba and Jinks characters are really wonderfully unique in
African-American literature, particularly in this mystery tale that is so
infused with so many intellectual ideas presented through the Frimbo and
Doctor Archer characters. Bubba Brown and Jinks Jenkins are the comic
relief. They are characters in that transitional phase, coming out of the minstrel period, sometimes called "coons." They are not. They are bona fide
comedic characters, three-dimensional, full of life, with fantastically clever
lines and many plays on words and spoonerisms. These characters also bridge
the vaudeville era.

There have been some critics who have likened Bubba and Jinks to
Laurel and Hardy. There are very specific references and descriptions in
the novel that one is short and rotund, the other is tall and lanky. I think
he is even called a string bean. If you think of the images of Laurel and
Hardy, you'll see them. They're very much realized in the Bubba and Jinks
characters.

They are two of the really very important engines of the play, providing
it with its wonderful sense of humor as well as a different point of view, a different aspect of the Harlem community. There were some critics who lam-
basted it because of the characters of Jinks and Bubba, but then, it was a
popular success. It appealed to such a broad segment of the population.

The metaphysical aspects of the production were also part of the discussion in intellectual circles—various aspects of cosmology and metaphysics as
they related to the African-American, as opposed to African or Caribbean
cosmology. Fisher has represented so many diverse aspects of the African
Diaspora.

In this play Frimbo comes back to life to help solve his murder. This orig-
inates in the Egyptian Osiris myth. He was cut up, his body dismembered, and
ultimately brought back and reassembled so he could come back to life and
solve his own murder. That discussion was very much alive during the Harlem
Renaissance.

Fisher was severely criticized by other well-known writers of the Harlem
Renaissance,[2] Countee Cullen among them, because he was presenting the
underbelly of Harlem life. There were many different movements in the
Harlem Renaissance as to what images of African-American should be por-

trayed. Langston Hughes was a wonderful advocate of Fisher and his work. He is quoted as saying that he really was always in amazement to be in Fisher's presence, because Fisher could always say some of the most clever things imaginable and leave Langston Hughes speechless. It's very interesting, because Rudolph Fisher is one of the writers that we don't hear that much about in the Harlem Renaissance.

This was a transitory period in black theatre, and there were amazing changes that were occurring with the support of the WPA and the Negro Theatre Unit. These plays provided tremendous employment for artists, actors, designers; helped transition into what I guess you would call the beginning of a more modern theatre movement, sloughing off the minstrel idiom— really a move from the vaudeville take of Bert Williams and those types of entertainers. This had a more literary bent to it.

One of the major legacies of the Federal Theatre Project and the Negro Units of the Federal Theatre Project was that it offered tremendous employment opportunities for African-American artists, gave voice to these artists, and made possible the growth that we have seen since the demise of the WPA. If you read the names of the artists who were involved in the Federal Theatre Project, not only African-Americans but whites as well, it reads like a Who's Who in American theatre, particularly those artists who got their start and then went on to become major stars in the fifties and sixties, like Canada Lee, Rose McClendon, Jack Carter, Rosetta LeNoire.

The Federal Theatre Project: I miss it, the idea of it. It served a wonderful purpose that needs to be reinvigorated.

❖   ❖   ❖

CLINTON TURNER DAVIS, *director of* Conjur Man Dies, *directed the acclaimed revival of August Wilson's* Joe Turner's Come and Gone *at the New Federal Theatre. Other award-winning productions include Athol Fugard's* My Children! My Africa! *(Dallas Theatre Center) and Langston Hughes's* Black Nativity *(Freedom Theatre),* Sweet 'n' Hot in Harlem *(Stage West), and* Trinidad Sisters *(Arena Stage). He is the cofounder of the Non-Traditional Casting Project, associate professor of drama at Colorado College, and associate producer for the New Federal Theatre.*

LINCOLN DIAMANT

FEDERAL THEATRE AUDIENCE MEMBER, NEW YORK

The audience was marching about five abreast up Seventh Avenue. People watching were wondering, What the hell is going on here? They had never seen a promotional stunt like this connected with the theatre. Oh, it was fantastic!

The Cradle Will Rock[3] was merely reflecting the general tone of how people felt in the country about a lot of important things. I count myself privileged 'cause I was able to go to a great number of shows when I was young. I had a little bit of pin money. I would see what I could in New York City. We were all sort of generally interested in moving the world forward.

The Federal Theatre under the WPA was set up very simply to take care of unemployed actors and actresses, set designers, and choreographers, to give them a place to work, 'cause very few people had work. In some places in the United States, on average about seventy-five percent of the people in the household were unable to work because there were no jobs. They saw their future crashing in around them.

The need for the Federal Theatre existed because it would satisfy audiences and it would satisfy the people on the stage who were working for their living, a good honest job. It represented what was going on in the United States.

I was born in 1923. The Stock Market Crash was in '29. The country was in a state of mass lockjaw. Nobody knew what to do. The breadlines were tremendously long. The Hoover Administration thought that the unemployed could be kept busy selling apples on every street corner. So, the question was where your next meal was coming from or how long a line you have to stand in to get it.

A lot of social dissention was centered in the larger cities in the United States. The unemployed, the jobless, and the homeless were all attacked physically in Washington by a U.S. Army group. Hoover ordered them, through General MacArthur, who was in charge of that operation with Lieutenant Colonel Eisenhower. They chased the Bonus Marchers out of Anacostia Park, where they'd set up a tar paper shack city—chased them back to where they came from in various parts of the United States. They did it with bayonets, and they did it with tear gas. They even used tanks. All the marchers wanted was a bonus promised to them by a congressional law in 1924. When they were not able to get the bonus, they figured a march on Washington, which has become traditional now.

Against this background, a young writer comes along like Marc Blitzstein, offering populist theatre. I'd like to describe the scene for you, just so you get a feeling of what it was like. It was a long time ago for me; I'm seventy-seven now.

THE NIGHT THE CRADLE ROCKED

That night in particular I went down with my mother. As we approached, there was this usual milling crowd that you find outside the theatre two or three minutes before the curtain's about to go up. It was the opening night of *Cradle Will Rock*, and nobody was scurrying in anywhere. They were just talking louder and louder in the group outside. A large, heavy brass chain that locked all the lobby doors together was in place, and nobody could get in. Federal marshals were guarding the stage door. It was not an auspicious beginning.

Somehow or other they had found another theatre—that was the Venice Theatre[4] up on Seventh Avenue just south of 59th Street, but you had ten blocks to go before you got there. An impromptu parade was organized. I can see somebody standing on a sidewalk in Times Square watching this parade go by. At the head was a truck. In the truck was a piano, and the truck was covered with posters for *Cradle Will Rock*. Sitting on a piano stool was Marc Blitzstein,[5] and he was playing songs from the show. The audience was marching about five abreast up Seventh Avenue. People watching were wondering, What the hell is going on here? They had never seen a promotional stunt like this connected with the theatre. Oh, it was fantastic!

Excitement was everywhere. Everybody was talking. When I went into the Venice Theatre, it was like a community meeting going on. Everybody's racing for seats and trying to get the best place they could sit and wondering how they were going to put on a play that had been banned by the government.

Let me try to describe the feeling in the theatre as the play started. There was no curtain pull; there was just this bare piano lit by a single spot. Blitzstein came out and sat down at the piano because he was going to play the musical accompaniment for the entire play, 'cause the musicians' union deserted. The usual level of sound tapers off, and Blitzstein began to play. He sounded the opening chords of *Cradle Will Rock*, and there was sort of quietness in the theatre that was unlike anything I'd ever seen at that time. He got to the first singing cue, which is "Nickel under My Foot," and as he was singing, a voice came out of the audience. She started singing alongside Blitzstein. He recognized what was happening, and he dropped away and let her continue to sing. It was this girl singing her lines. He gave the follow spot an opportunity to see where she was and pick her up. You can do a play that way. I know because I was there; it happened.

Bit by bit, the other singers chimed in, and pretty soon Blitzstein was doing nothing but playing, and the whole cast spotted throughout the audience just sort of had everybody's heart in their mouth. It was the kind of thing you don't find ordinarily. It was the kind of thing that makes you remember a long time.

When he finally came to the spot in the curtain calls that was his alone on the stage, the place went wild. The actors were not named, but they would stand up in rotation, depending on where they were in the theatre, and each received a round of applause. I really can't remember a theatre audience quite as delirious.

I remember the music most of all. It was somewhat atonal. It was a new sound. This young man up on the stage who was playing his heart out never had that particular kind of an audience. He'd been a writer, a songwriter, a poet, and musician.

After the last note sounded, everybody turned to his neighbor and started talking a mile a minute. There were still people out in front in the lobby arguing the play when [the authorities] came to shut down the theatre.[6] [The audience members had] been out there an hour just talking, talking.

In my conversation with John Houseman about fifty years later, I said, "You know, I was part of the original audience that walked up Seventh Avenue to the Venice Theatre for the opening of *The Cradle Will Rock*." He said to me in his professorial, Harvard Law voice, "Well, you're only one of thousands." Apparently, everybody in the world was identifying themselves to John Houseman as being in the audience.

❖   ❖   ❖

LINCOLN DIAMANT, *in addition to being a lover of theatre, is a historian of the Revolutionary War and an author of books about Hudson Valley history. A former CBS newswriter and advertising executive, he has written numerous books on the American Revolution, including* Bernard Romans: Forgotten Patriot of the American Revolution *and* Chaining the Hudson: The Fight for the River in the American Revolution.

RICHARD EYRE

FORMER DIRECTOR, NATIONAL THEATRE OF GREAT BRITAIN

I think that the Federal Theatre Project, with hindsight, was the most extraordinary phenomenon in American cultural history. It had no precedent, and it has had no successor—I think much to the detriment of American theatre.

I think it's important, if you believe in government funding, that you have to accept that you are creating an agency that is endowing people with funds that may boomerang. What you're saying to people is, Art is everything that politics isn't. Art is wayward; it's passionate. It's all about ambiguity of feelings, whereas politics is all about certainty. You won't get a politician ever to say, "Well, I'm not sure about this," whereas the whole essence of art is that that's what it does. It tries to put together a picture of the world through looking at it from many different angles. So, it's an absolute inevitability if you endow art, any good art is in some sense a criticism. They are licensing the jester, at best.

"ART IS ALL ABOUT THE I, THE INDIVIDUAL"

I think that the U.S. government has understood all too well that it is a consequence of art that you enfranchise people, the very people who you find most irritating. The people whose private lives may be even messier than politicians and who are explicitly critical of the status quo and particularly of corporate America. Art is all about the I, the individual. That's inherently the enemy of corporations and government, which are to do with masses of people. None of us want to be criticized by the people to whom we're being generous.

In this country [Great Britain] there is a genuine belief that society is better for a diversity of viewpoints and in some way it's the responsibility of government. It's a responsibility of government to fund arts and cultural events because it's part of the fabric of life. In some way it enriches everybody's lives even if only a narrow sector of society can be seen visibly as the beneficiary.

To make a case for the usefulness of art is rather dangerous because you end up pursuing a sort of utilitarian argument which has to do with community values and keeping people occupied so that they don't get into trouble, or that in some way it's a sort of tax benefit. You put money into the arts, and eventually, you'll get money back in taxes. I think these are specious and reductive arguments. I think that patrons of all forms for the arts, public and private, should accept that art is its own justification, that you can't quantify it. One of the ways in which you define art is by saying you can't put a value on it, and of course, people love to put value on it. They love to say, "This painting is worth . . . ." But actually, paintings aren't worth anything except under the feelings and thoughts they invoke in the watcher. It's the same with audiences for plays.

I did a play at the National Theatre by David Hare about the three estates. The three estates in the seventeenth century were the church, the law, and the government. *The Absence of War* was a play about an opposition party, which is the Labour Party. The play was heavily critical in that it indicted the Labour Party for not knowing really what they believed in and why they believed it. It was an even more powerful indictment of the Tory Party that was then in power for believing in nothing, behaving in an entirely unprincipled fashion. There's a good many plays about public affairs that are highly critical of the government of the day. So, it wasn't a great novelty to be presenting *The Absence of War* and saying, Look: Both parties deserve to be criticized, and the party in power more profoundly criticized than the party aspiring to power.

In the seventies when I was running a regional theatre, virtually every new play of any quality—and some of them were of tremendous quality—were revolutionary. Tectonic plates in society were really moving. In the sixties and seventies, we believed that some profound change in society was required. We were demanding it, and often the forum was the sort of plays that were describing people's lives and demonstrating how people's lives could be changed.

The huge irony for us of course is that the change came in the eighties, and it came in exactly the opposite direction to which we were exhorting our audience to move. As Orson Welles said, "Poetry makes nothing happen."

A profound indictment of the American lack of public funding was the play *Angels in America* by Tony Kushner, which is a two-part play and lasts seven hours. Now, that play came to me via Gordon Davidson, who runs the Mark Taper Theatre in Los Angeles. He said, "You know, there's this great piece of writing. Are you interested?" I was two pages in before I decided to present the play. We presented the first part at the National Theatre fifteen months before it went on in New York, before it first had a proper, a major, professional production in the United States. It's a revolutionary play in that it really does say, "Just look at your society." It covers religion and sexuality and the notion of the coming of the Apocalypse in an extraordinarily complex and subversive way. I would say that was the most explicitly subversive play that I put on during my time at the National Theatre.

If you ask me, "Why does theatre need subsidy?" I would say because the subsidized theatre is there to do what can't be done in the commercial theatre or what won't be done in the commercial theatre, or what could be done in the commercial theatre in a way that would never be done in the commercial theatre. Apart from which, subsidy allows you to keep your seat prices down, which means that you do have a possibility of democratizing your audience.

Commercial theatre exists to make money. That's fine; there's nothing wrong with that. Subsidized theatre exists to be good. Now, of course, somebody in the commercial theatre will say, "Well, we want to do good theatre, too." Yes, but that's not the first priority. The first priority of commercial theatre is the law of gravity, of commerce. You make a profit. You have to make money.

In the subsidized theatre your responsibility is to be good first. In order to create the conditions in which that imperative can be maintained, you need subsidy because you need continuity of investment. If your subsidy is so low that you become a sort of quasi-commercial organization because you're so dependent on your success not to be able to take risks, every play you put on, commercial or subsidized, is a huge risk. You send out the invitations to the party, and you wait to see if anybody turns up. A lot of the time, they don't.

Subsidized theatre is an artificial economy. You create an economy which breeds success and which allows for failure. A government can justify it by saying, "In the end you are pursuing something which is for the value of all, for the collective good."

If you're gonna encourage people to go to the theatre, if you're gonna keep the medium of theatre alive, you need to enfranchise those people who simply can't spend ninety dollars to go to a play. Who can? Nobody complains if public money goes into sporting facilities. Nobody complains if public money goes into building of concert halls or libraries or galleries. So why should people complain about funding the art form of theatre?

In this country there is a principle, which is built into the Constitution, of public funding of the arts. It's known as the arm's-length principle. What happens is the government department responsible for cultural affairs, cultural and sporting and broadcasting affairs, gives money to an autonomous body called the Arts Council. The Arts Council is composed of people who are appointed by the government but are encouraged to be independent. It is an autonomous body. The job of the Arts Council is to receive an allocation from the government and to act as an evangelical body on behalf of the arts.

If you look at these European countries, they are saying, "We subsidize art because we want to boast that we have the greatest theatre company, the greatest ballet company." Do you hear any Americans say, "I wish to give money to the arts in order that I can boast that America is the greatest country in the world in the field of playwriting"?

The hardest thing for governments, for patrons of any form, is to accept that if you're funding an art form, there is absolutely no guarantee that what you fund will be good. You cannot legislate the quality or talent, and that's at the heart of the problem. People want linear equations. They want to be able to say, "We put in X million dollars; we get this out the other end."

THE FEDERAL THEATRE PROJECT

The Federal Theatre Project—we can look at it now and say this was a fantastic, benign, brilliant project. You know, there were ten thousand people involved in the Federal Theatre Project at its peak. There were millions of people who went to the theatre, who enjoyed the theatre for the first time in their lives. There were massive quantities of bad plays, bad performances, bad art. Now is that in itself an argument against the Federal Theatre Project? In my view not, because it's like mining for diamonds, you know, or panning for gold. You simply don't stop the practice because it takes, you know, three years and sifting the grit, and you come up with a gold nugget.

It's a tragedy, I think, that the Federal Theatre Project stopped. I'm not saying it wasn't possible to revive a similar system. Such was the chronic fear of the virus of socialism, of communism, that any initiative for the public good was stamped on. In my view an absolute, unambiguous tragedy for the American theatre is that its subsidy was withdrawn with the end of the Federal Theatre Project.

❖   ❖   ❖

SIR RICHARD EYRE (b. 1943) *is one of the leading voices of the British theatre. He is the former artistic director of the Royal National Theatre. He has directed numerous classics and new plays as well as the BAFTA award–winning BBC drama* Tumbledown. *He recently published* Changing Stages: A View of British Theatre in the Twentieth Century.

PART 5 NOTES

[1]**Rudolph Fisher** is considered one of the major literary figures of the Harlem Renaissance. A true Renaissance man, Fisher was a physician, novelist, dramatist, musician, and orator. His acclaimed novel *The Walls of Jericho* (1928) presents a cross section of life in Harlem, as does his novel *The Conjure-Man Dies: A Mystery Tale of Dark Harlem*.

[2]Harlem Renaissance writers, musicians, and playwrights—such as **Langston Hughes, Countee Cullen,** and **Zora Neale Hurston**—chronicled the social history of Harlem in the 1920s and 1930s.

[3]*The Cradle Will Rock* is a musical satire in two acts set in Steeltown, U.S.A. According to the *New York Times*, it was "a tale of big industry corruption and labor union gallantry," although it took on everything from religion and art to medicine and education. Its opening coincided with violent steel labor strikes throughout the country, forcing the government to place a ban on all new productions. The stark, simple power of the minimal staging and music broke new theatrical ground.

[4]**The Venice Theatre,** also known as the Century Theatre, was located at 932 Seventh Avenue between 58th and 59th Streets. It was built by the Shuberts for Al Jolson and closed during the Depression. It stood vacant until the night of June 16, 1937, when it was commandeered for the production of *The Cradle Will Rock*. It reopened formally in 1944.

[5]**Marc Blitzstein** (1905–1964), a talented and innovative composer, lyricist, and librettist, was best known for his socially relevant work *The Cradle Will Rock*. Born in Philadelphia, he trained with Nadia Boulanger in Paris and Arnold Schoenberg in Berlin. He translated and adapted Bertolt Brecht's *The Three-Penny Opera* (1952), an off-Broadway success. Other works include *The Airborne Symphony* (1946), *Regina* (1949), *Reuben, Reuben* (1955), and *Juno* (1959).

[6]Orson Welles's and John Houseman's Project 891 opened **The Cradle Will Rock** in defiance of a federal order that there was to be "no new productions" by the Federal Theatre Project of the WPA. Equity had told its members that they could not take part in the show. They got around this by sitting in the audience and rising to sing when cued by Blitzstein at the piano. Shortly after, Welles and Houseman left the Federal Theatre to found their new Mercury Theatre, where *The Cradle Will Rock* opened officially on December 6, 1937, still without costumes and scenery. As legend has it, this minimal approach became a gimmick, with Blitzstein continuing to conduct, announce, and play various roles throughout the opera.

It moved to Broadway, opening January 4, 1938, with Will Geer again playing Mr. Mister, Howard Da Silva as Larry Foreman, and Hiram Sherman as Reverend Salvation. The Broadway house required union musicians, and it was agreed that a band of ten would be hired. On opening night they sat in the audience. There was no orchestra in the pit, and Marc Blitzstein continued to play solo.

Conjur Man Dies, Lafayette Theatre, New York, 1936,
Bubba and Jinks

Fritz Weller as Frimbo in *Conjur Man Dies*, Lafayette
Theatre, New York, 1936

Lincoln Diamant, New York, 2000

Marc Blitzstein at *The Cradle Will Rock* rehearsal, New York, 1937

The Cradle Will Rock cast with Marc Blitzstein, 1937

Richard Eyre, London, 2001

BONNIE NELSON SCHWARTZ is a producer in theatre, film, and television. She has worked on more than one hundred plays, films, television programs, specials, and concerts in Washington, D.C., New York, and London. On Broadway she coproduced *Pack of Lies*, starring Rosemary Harris and Patrick McGoohan; *Ian McKellan: Acting Shakespeare*; *Jerome Kern Goes to Hollywood*; and Rodgers and Hammerstein's *State Fair* with the Theatre Guild. Her off-Broadway credits include *Dylan Thomas: Return Journey*, directed by Anthony Hopkins, and *Babalooney*.

Ms. Schwartz is the creator and original producer of Washington, D.C.'s Helen Hayes Awards. She produced the Atlanta portion of the closing ceremonies for the 1992 Olympic Games in Barcelona. For the 1996 Atlanta Olympic Games, she cocreated and produced *The Olympic Woman*, a multimedia exhibition, with book and videos, on the history of women in the Olympic Games. Recent productions include *Give My Regards to Broadway: 125 Years of the Musical Theatre* at Carnegie Hall; the London production of *Panbeaters*, a play with music; and *In Concert against Hate: A Tribute to the Heroes of 9/11* with the National Symphony Orchestra.

Ms. Schwartz is currently coproducing an independent feature film in South Africa, based on Nobel laureate Nadine Gordimer's book *My Son's Story*, and a television special, *Harlem in Paris*.

INDEX

Page numbers in boldface refer to photographs.